D0579620

GROW A LIVING WALL

CREATE VERTICAL GARDENS WITH PURPOSE

Pollinators • Herbs and Veggies • Aromatherapy • Many More

SHAWNA CORONADO

COOL
SPRINGS
PRESS
Home and Garden Experts™
MINNEAPOLIS, MINNESOTA

CONTENTS

7
Introduction
How to Make a Difference with a Living Wall

Part I
*How to Create
Living Walls*

22
Which Living Wall System
Is Right for You?

26
Tools That Help

29
Getting Started

31
Watering the Living Wall

32
Soil and Compost

35
Choosing and Obtaining Plants
for Your Living Wall

Part II
*Living Wall Gardens
with Purpose*

43
Herbal Cocktail Garden
*A Freestanding Herb Garden Planted
with Mixology in Mind*

47
Moss and Shade Wall Art
*Low-Maintenance Moss Makes a Novel
Design Statement in Any Home*

51
Vegetable "Balconies" Garden
*These Hanging Veggie Boxes Deliver
Fresh Food and Fresh Air*

55
Fern Garden
*A Stunning Vertical Wall Solution for
Shady and Damp Locations*

59
Cactus Living Wall
*Put a Spotlight on Exotic Desert Beauty and Color
with an Arrangement of Water-Smart Cactus*

65
Therapeutic Hanging Gardens
*Two Simple Living Wall Arrangements that Turn
a Plain Gate into a Calming Garden Element*

73
Hydroponic Pollinator Garden
*This Beautiful (and Soilless) Flowering Garden Offers
Food and Shelter for Bees and Butterflies*

79
Shade Pallet Garden
Bringing New Life to a Living Wall Using Some Old Wood

83
Insulate-a-Wall Garden
Use Flowers, Vegetables, and Herbs to Save Energy

89
Bookshelf Fence Garden
Upcycle an Old Bookshelf into a Shady Living Wall

93
Succulent Living Wall
*These Fleshy Plants Are More Popular than Ever,
Plus They're Perfect for a Living Wall*

97
Vertical Vegetable Farm
*Grow Luscious, Fresh Veggies
Even in the Tiniest Spaces*

101
Aphrodisiac Wall Garden
Grow Your Own Garden of Love

107
Freestanding Entrance Garden
*A Pretty Project to Improve Curb Appeal
with Houseplants*

113
Culinary Kitchen Garden
*Grow Your Own Organic Vegetables and
Herbs for Cooking*

119
Aromatherapy Garden
*Invite Some Favorite Scents into Your Garden
to Improve Mood*

125
Money-Saving Garden
*Growing a Fruitful Garden from Seed
Is Practically Free*

131
Smart Garden
*A Balcony Garden Can Help Increase Your
Attention Span in Your Home Office*

135
Colorful Living Wall
Build One Today Because Beauty Is Important

139
Vitamin-Rich Culinary Garden
Fresh Herbs and Vegetables at Your Fingertips

143
Urban Water-Saving Garden
Conserve Water and Make a Difference

148
Living Wall Maintenance

152
Online Product Resources

153
Contributors

155
Acknowledgments

156
Conversions

157
Index

160
Meet Shawna Coronado

INTRODUCTION

How to Make a Difference with a Living Wall

IMAGINE A REVOLUTIONARY PLANTING technique that lets you plant more than thirty plants in a floor area that is only one square foot. The trick is simply to grow up, not out. Gardening with this technique is amazingly simple and easy to accomplish for anyone, just by planting a living wall garden. Sited on fences, gates, walls, balconies, and even doors, living wall gardens save enormous amounts of space, while producing an abundance of flowers, perennials, herbs, and vegetables.

I came up with the idea of planting more vertical or living walls on my own property when I picked up a 24-by-7-inch window box, did a little math, and discovered that its footprint was exactly 1.16 square feet. Then I thought: What if I stacked five window boxes on top of one another and fastened them to the wall? That 1.16-square-foot garden would increase its planting capacity five times. In about one square foot of floor space, I could plant nearly 6 square feet of plants. This would enable me to plant between thirty-five and forty-five plants. How's that for efficient? And what if small-space gardeners all over the world would adopt this vertical growing method? That would mean more food for the hungry and more flowering plants for pollinators. Planting vertically could truly help a family make a difference for themselves and their community.

What else can living walls do? They can help save energy and reduce utility expenses, solve challenging design issues, mitigate urban heat issues, inspire therapeutic living, grow aphrodisiac plants, contribute to your culinary kitchen, save water, help beautify a community, help save the pollinating insects, and even help you entertain your friends. Do you love herbal tea? Design a garden with all the herbs you need to make your favorite herbal tea blends. Imagine having a cute little kitchen garden or cocktail herb garden that can reside right on your balcony or patio. The point is, these distinct, self-contained gardens are just the right size to make any statement or develop any theme you want, from the frivolous to the life-affirming. With a living wall you can make a difference by creating something that is both attractive and useful.

While the practical applications for living wall gardens are virtually unlimited, for many people the best reason to grow one is simply that they are beautiful and truly artistic conversation pieces.

← Are you concerned about bees and colony collapse? Why not design a lovely, flowering pollinator wall that attracts bees and butterflies and gives them a safe refuge? This is a great example of what I mean when I say "vertical gardens with purpose."

Living walls offer brilliant solutions, such as creating privacy for home gardens by blocking neighbor sightlines into patios and balconies. *Plant Connection, Inc.*

What IS a Living Wall?

A living wall is a self-sufficient vertical garden growing on the side of a building, fence, gate, or balcony. Within the living wall system is a structural support that is fastened directly to the supporting wall or fence that holds the plant roots and soil system. It can be soil-based or water-based, and some have built-in watering systems. Plants receive their nutrients from within the vertical structural support system. Garden walls that have plants with their roots in the ground, such as walls filled with ivy or covered with honeysuckle, are not considered a living wall.

Several other terms are used to describe a living wall. For example, *green wall* is a common synonym for a living wall system. Other names include ecowall, biowall, hydrowall, vegetated wall, plant wall, or vertical garden. Within this book you will see both *living wall* and *vertical wall garden* used interchangeably to mean the same thing: most typically a garden that can be attached to a wall or fence of some kind or even function as a standalone multi-tiered garden that is not directly attached to a wall at all. Living walls are remarkably versatile and afford the ability to grow in spaces that are much smaller than the traditional garden.

More Fun, Less Work

Most living walls require far less work than traditional in-the-ground gardening. There is no weeding involved. Gardeners everywhere jump up and cheer—no weeding is a reason to celebrate!

Living walls can save you a lot of time. Many of the new living wall products have self-watering systems to automate your watering. If they do not come with a watering system, it is easy to install one for your particular living wall situation. Because you will spend less time weeding and watering, you will have more time to do important things like read a book or drink herbal martinis with your friends or bike the Yukon.

Another benefit of vertical wall gardening is that it is out of reach of many garden pests; it is pretty tough for a rabbit to climb a 6-foot wall and munch on lettuce. Some insect pests can only get at the plants when they physically contact the ground, and living walls are often hung well above ground level. While growing a living wall does not guarantee that bad insects will stay away, chances are that you will see fewer ground-related insects. A positive twist on this is that you will very likely see more flying pollinators such as bees and butterflies, which you want to encourage for stronger flower and vegetable production.

Living walls are amazingly versatile and can be planted in virtually any location outdoors that offers even the slightest direct or indirect light exposure. Did you know that you can grow vegetables in the shade? In this book you will find lists of shade and sun plants that you can choose from to have the best success with your particular living wall situation.

One of the most rewarding and fantastic benefits of having a living wall at home is the reaction from your friends and family. Every friend who comes to visit my yard is fascinated with the gardens on my walls; they want their own wall garden, and they also want to learn how it might help them make a difference. My daughters have loved the vertical wall gardens, and in turn, the gardens have become educational tools to help my children find their health, learn to enjoy nature by getting their hands dirty planting, and learn about the environmental impact of things such as pollinators. Simply by having a living wall, you are creating an educational tool that has an impact on others.

Easy Sustainable Choices

Living walls have a great impact because they also serve a higher sustainable purpose for you and the environment. Doing things that are good for the planet is far more than a trend; it is the heart and soul of a community. In modern-day media and advertising, deceptive "greenwashing" campaigns have caused a lot of confusion about what we can do sustainably as individuals to make a difference for ourselves and the environment. Grand life changes with giant projects attached to them are lovely and all, but they're usually not practical for most of us. How can we make a difference for our communities at a level that is practical and easier to accomplish? I want everyone to feel that they can do something good for themselves and their neighbors within their daily lives. This book focuses on how we can create practical, sustainable, purposeful, and manageable gardens in small spaces.

There are many reasons why living walls can be a sustainable part of your family's environment. When we grow plants of any kind, we are restricted by the hardiness zone issue. For example, some plants, such as tropicals, don't do well in cooler regions. But when you plant a living wall garden, you are tapping into the warmth of the wall. This can raise your garden's climactic conditions a few degrees, which could be all it takes for you to be able to grow new varieties of plants or even extend your growing season. Wall growing also can have a heat-reducing effect inside the home by limiting direct sun exposure and heat absorption. And there are many more environmentally friendly reasons to grow a living wall, such as air quality improvement, noise mitigation, health considerations, energy efficiency, and a connection with nature.

With paint and upcycled materials, an urban living wall can be a bold and colorful statement on an unused and underappreciated wall. *Danielle Wieland of www.stacykfloral.com*

Every season I tour all around the country, educating communities on how to garden. This "purposeful" living wall book idea was inspired by the repeated and pointed questions I receive from attendees at my speaking events. Without fail, I get the very same questions over and over: "How do I grow a healthy garden for my family when I have very little space and a lack of garden know-how?" or "How can I make a difference with a garden?" This book is meant to address these issues as well as discuss the reason to start gardening in the first place: because a garden is always certainly more than *just* a garden.

Why Should Everyone Garden?

I think everyone on the planet should grow a garden. Whether it's a living wall, a raised garden, or an in-ground garden, a garden has benefits that can be significant and important to you as an individual and to your community.

- Gardening is fun.
- Vegetable and herb gardening can save your family money and provide food for local food pantries.
- Gardens of all kinds improve the value of your home and property.
- Landscaping and gardens can reduce crime.

- Therapeutic gardening, and spending time outdoors in general, improves depression and overall health.
- Growing organic food can reduce a family's chemical consumption.
- Gardens improve air quality.
- Gardens help the health of our bees and pollinators by providing a food and housing source for them.
- Building a garden can improve the heat island effect in urban areas, reducing the city's heat off put.
- Saving energy is possible by wall gardening; it reduces home energy use.

↑ Boring brick walls in urban areas can be improved by adding living walls. Dull, unattractive neighborhoods in heavy urban areas often have blank brick walls just waiting for a living wall to be placed. Sharing a garden, whether it be edible or tropical or anything in between, is sharing hope for the future with your community.

→ Building a beautiful setting with a living wall can increase home value and reduce crime in urban communities. This display garden at Ball Horticultural Company in West Chicago, Illinois, demonstrates the experience of a living wall when enhanced with flower container displays.

Vertical gardens can be found on walls, gates, and even doors (or even indoors, for that matter). This living door at Longwood Gardens Conservatory in Kennett Square, Pennsylvania, is filled with tillandsia. These low-maintenance air plants give the door an intriguing fantasy aspect.

Living walls are a marvelous way to grow more culinary herbs and foods in less space, thereby creating a small-space solution that can make a big difference. This living wall at the Chicago Botanic Garden in Illinois is filled with herbs.

Why Living Walls?

An important subset of traditional gardening, living walls can be grown in very narrow and small spaces because they grow upward (or downward in some cases). Therefore, it is possible to have a smaller footprint, but a significantly larger yield. This offers an answer to anyone who is concerned that she or he has no space to grow: if you have a wall, you have a space. Vertical wall space can be found in heavily urban areas, in traditional suburban neighborhoods, and in the country on fences, garages, gates, and barns. That small vertical space can be available whether you are a renter or homeowner, professional gardener, or someone who has never gardened before.

Living walls offer a remarkable, practical small-space solution no matter where you choose to grow vertically. Whether it be on a fence, on a gate or door, on a wall, or on a balcony, living walls can be an astounding solution for a family seeking a healthier and greener lifestyle. Living walls that are purposeful as well as beautiful contribute to your lifestyle in a positive way.

Why Do I Garden?

I first learned that gardening has many health and environmental benefits during the year I left my fancy-pants corporate job and started doing landscape design for a living. I spent that summer outdoors in the sunshine building gardens of all sorts. Without a doubt, every day I came home sore and tired but happy as a clam. At the beginning of that summer, I took over a dozen prescriptions per day trying to cope with all of my allergies, year-round bronchitis, and stress-related health issues. By the end of my first summer gardening, I had gone down to two prescriptions per day and felt like a million bucks. The time I spent growing became a truly life-changing experience for me personally and spurred me to consider social good as an integral part of the growing experience.

This change in my health was the result of spending time outside touching nature and working to make my life as chemical-free as possible, while living a practical urban lifestyle with my family. Growing and eating foods that contain fewer chemicals was an important step toward better health for me. The simple act of planting and growing in any situation can be mind-freeing and help all aspects of your physical health. Gardening is fun, and being outside touching plants in a nurturing way is a part of that pleasurable experience.

About This Book

Each vertical garden chapter in this book addresses a need or a purpose that helps you or the environment. Below is a list of ideas that will be covered in the book, which all offer very practical, purposeful, and easy-growing concepts:

- Build a pollinator feeding station to help save the bees.
- Create a nurturing and therapeutic garden that promotes healing.
- Grow vegetables in shade or sun that have high vitamin and nutrition content.
- Recycle and reuse items such as a pallet or an old bookshelf to make a vertical garden.
- Use living walls as an herbal resource for cocktail and culinary uses.

- Save energy with a living wall, as it insulates walls and helps cancel noise.
- Save water by using a vertical wall garden as a beautiful, drought-tolerant growing solution.
- Use vertical gardens in urban areas as a tool to increase air quality near windows and entrances.

Growing a living wall is more than growing living art; it can make a difference for you and your family. These weed-free, small-space gardens have an exceptional amount of personality and usefulness. Growing a sustainable and healthy living wall is easy to do with far-reaching, practical returns for all who try the technique. Use this book as a how-to that will introduce you to the fun and joy of growing a living wall.

Vertical gardens can be artistic as well as useful. This lovely living wall garden is situated on an urban home patio as a way to beautify the wall and add a unique contribution to the outdoor room design. *Plant Connection, Inc.*

↑ Living walls have become a fantastic solution for public spaces, offering more oxygenated air and green space than an area that is gardened with a flat perspective. *Photo courtesy of Copley Wolff Design Group and photographer Luke O'Neill*

→ While most living walls are tightly planted so that more plants grow in a small space, some living walls are designed simply for beauty. This wall at Xel-Ha Eco-Park in Mexico is a living wall with the plants floating at wider intervals. It demonstrates that understatement and simplicity can be an intricate part of a beautiful display.

↑ In her garden near Atlantic City, New Jersey, Liz Donaghy has created an artistic herb garden masterpiece right outside the back door. She combines a wall garden with a raised bed in a small-space area that grows an abundance of culinary delights.

→ Side yards can be used as intensive growing areas where large quantities of herbs, vegetables, and pollinator plants can be grown in a narrow space area. These gardens, which grow in seemingly boring areas of our properties, can become attractive as well as useful.

→ Many different types of systems and containers can be used to support a living wall garden design. Here is a gorgeous wall of flowering orchids at the Longwood Gardens Conservatory in Kennett Square, Pennsylvania.

↑ Living walls vary from full-wall infrastructures to structurally simple and utilitarian, as in the case of this children's wall garden at the Brookfield Zoo in Brookfield, Illinois.

→ Outdoor kitchens have become all the rage in many parts of the world. Growing living walls both for embellishment purposes and for providing herbs and other culinary treats can improve property value. *Plant Connection, Inc.*

↑ Growing a combination of herbs and vegetables together in a living wall feeds the family and is an edible delight to the eye, particularly when planted on an unattractive fence.

← Have a dull, underappreciated area on your back balcony or patio that needs spicing up? Colorful flowers on a vertical living wall are a fantastic way to add a natural spark of sunshine. *Plant Connection, Inc.*

→ Foliage plants can make remarkably colorful additions to a living wall garden. Various types of begonia, coleus, and tropical plants can be combined for a spectacular display as seen here at Ball Horticultural Company in West Chicago, Illinois.

↓ This growing fence at the Chicago Botanic Garden is a living wall formed from various drought-tolerant sedums. It brings color as well as structure to a busy pathway.

↑ Incorporating vertical wall systems into an ornamental edible garden can help you grow more edibles and also add interest to the garden. This vegetable and edible flower view was discovered at the Chicago Botanic Garden.

↑ While most living walls are attached to large structures, some living walls, such as this planted arbor wall, can be added as the perfect miniature kitchen herb garden. *Plant Connection, Inc.*

↑ Growing massive numbers of plants in a smaller area can bring a lot of happiness to your locality. Living walls can improve health, reduce crime, feed the hungry, beautify a community, and support pollinators. Building a living wall can provide a solution for gardening in extremely small spaces that can truly make a difference for your neighborhood and the world.

Finding the right living wall system to fit your unique planting requirements will help you succeed at growing. This vista shows a shady, damp side yard filled with fern and moss living walls built for the local growing conditions. Learn how to grow a living wall before it is installed for the best success!

PART I

HOW TO CREATE LIVING WALLS

GETTING STARTED ON GROWING your first living wall is amazingly easy. Living wall gardens have a lot of the same needs as traditional container gardens. Therefore, succeeding with a living wall or vertical garden is as simple as choosing the right container, the right location, and the right plants. Having the ability to plant thirty-five to forty plants in an area that is less than 2 square feet offers an astounding amount of garden ideas for small space or urban growers.

Throughout this book you will see twenty-three complete living walls presented as individual gardening projects. Each wall is designed for a unique and specific purpose that goes beyond simply being beautiful. For example, one design will help you save energy by insulating walls and blocking heat. Other gardens are created to generate large quantities of food for you and your community. Versatility and practicality are two hallmarks of the living wall, and knowing why you want to grow a garden and for what purpose is as important as selecting the right system and plants.

Before we get to these creative designs, the following section will introduce you to the basic tools, materials, techniques, and know-how that you'll need for any living wall project, regardless of its purpose or unique properties. You'll find the information in the following six sections:

- Which Living Wall System Is Right for You?
- Tools That Help
- Getting Started
- Watering the Living Wall
- Soil and Compost
- Choosing and Obtaining Plants for Your Living Wall

WHICH LIVING WALL SYSTEM IS RIGHT FOR YOU?

THERE ARE MANY TYPES of living wall systems that you can utilize, and it is important to discover the living wall system that is right for you, your family, and your community. Several of these are "plug-and-play" products that are easily assembled; others are more homemade and are customized to your own wishes and standards. Choosing which type of system is best for you should be based on the size of the area where you plan to plant, the types of plants you are interested in, and the varying types of walls you have access to.

For many years, the term "green wall" meant that the roots of the plants existed in a soilless product of some kind, which was then hung on either an exterior or interior wall. In recent years, this definition has changed and expanded as more systems and units have come out for varying purposes. Living wall or green wall can be defined simply as a wall of plants with various types of soilless or soil-filled products supporting it.

Typically, there are four styles of living wall systems that are suitable for exterior living walls: mat systems, block systems, loose-medium systems, and homemade systems. No matter which style of living wall you choose, each can have a self-watering arrangement incorporated into it. This means fewer watering concerns and more ease of maintenance.

Mat-style systems are most frequently made from felt mats, coir fiber, or a rock substrate, much like the units

↑ Building a system for a living wall can be as simple as putting two nails in the wall and hanging a premade container, such as these lengths of gutter trough. Creating your own living wall from upcycled materials is one of the great joys of living wall gardening. Choosing which living wall concept is best for you is determined by the time and effort you would like to put into the project.

→ Hanging pocket systems have wool-like pockets sometimes made from recycled plastic. Finding a system that offers the potential to be beautiful and sustainable might be a smart choice for your family.

↑ Discovering the best system for your particular living wall can make the difference between success and failure for your vertical garden. For your needs, a standalone, manufactured system could be the answer.

↑ Framed living wall units are often smaller but serve as an excellent small-space living wall for balconies or patios where space is an issue.

used in the Freestanding Entrance Garden or the Pollinator Garden projects. Some, such as the Pollinator Garden, are exclusively hydroponic. Rooted plants are inserted into the system and most typically grow directly into the matting, which makes it a system that is less dependent on soil and more dependent on proper watering with organic fertilizer added to the water to help support the root structure. If left up too long, the mat system can become clogged with roots, which prevents proper watering, so the system should be refreshed regularly. Mat systems are best suited for installations that are smaller than 10 feet tall and wide in order to have easy access to repair planting pockets.

Block systems are highly structural. They are often shaped like bricks or blocks and sometimes combine soil and coir or other fiber into a heavy-duty planting brick. They are tough systems that can last up to fifteen years after they're installed. They are easy to replace for maintenance concerns. Block systems are the best choice in areas where earthquakes and seismic activity exist, because they build a more stable living wall. Many industrial living walls are created with block systems and, generally, they are less suitable for home use. The planting details of this particular system are not covered in this book due to its more industrial nature.

Loose-medium systems are the best solution for the everyday homeowner or community garden and are the principle systems featured in each project. They are built for installations that are less than 10 feet tall and have soil as the major base component for planting. Window box systems, pocket systems, bag systems, bracket-hung framed art pockets, and container-on-the-wall systems are all variations on the loose-medium concept. Loose-medium systems must have their soil/growing medium replaced once a season. Refreshing the soil is typically done in the early spring for most garden zones, particularly areas that have extreme winter garden weather. This enables the young plants to get a fresh start with clean rooting material.

Additional systems include homemade soilless concepts, such as the Moss and Shade Wall Art project—a do-it-yourself art concept that has no soil requirement whatsoever. Additionally, soil-filled bottles, jars, pallets, bookshelves, and other repurposed items can be reused to make a living wall unit.

Most living wall systems must be hung on a gate, fence, or wall. However, several of the living walls discussed in this book can be installed as standalone structures, yet are still classified as vertical systems because they are vertical standing container units that function as a wall unit. Apartment dwellers with small balconies or renters with tiny patios might consider the standalone systems for occasions where they do not want to or are not allowed to drill into the walls or fences of their building property.

Types of Systems

In this book, we demonstrate how to use several varieties of planting systems. Here is a list of the basic living wall unit styles.

- **Felt Wrap Living Wall**. This system involves wrapping a plant's rootball with a felt-like wrapper. The wrapper encloses the root system and enables you to insert it into the larger supportive system that hangs on a wall. The back of the living wall is made of plastic, so the wall is less likely to become damaged from water exposure. Each felt-wrapped plant can be pulled out and replaced for easy maintenance.

- **Hydroponic Soilless System**. This system is made from a BioTile, which is an independent rock fiber system that enables the gardener to grow the plants placed in the tile in a solely hydroponic fashion. An advantage of the system is the flat growing surface against the wall, which makes artistic planting designs appear to be a part of the wall.

- **Window Box Living Wall**. Window box living walls are just what they sound like: window box planting containers that have been stacked one on top of the other to create a planting system. These systems are remarkably easy to use because they can be handled like a traditional container garden and they only take up between 1 to 2 square feet of floor space. They can be hung on the wall, fence, or gate, or used as a standalone living wall. A perfect solution for urban areas and small-space gardening.

- **Planting Pocket Systems**. Pocket systems are usually made of a felt or fiber. Some have been made from recycled water bottles. Their pockets hold the soil and either seeds or plants can be planted in the soil pockets directly. Watering is unique as it is important to water the back tongue of the wall pocket at the top of each pocket entrance so that the fiber is thoroughly moistened.

- **Bracket-Hung Framed Art Walls**. Increasingly popular as a small-area solution, bracket-hung framed art pockets are really single polymer units that hold enough plants to build a small garden. With an artistic-looking frame, these units look great outside or in rooms that feature plant solutions. Each planting pocket area is lined with a moisture-holding felt mat. Fill the pocket area with soil, then water from the top.

- **Modular Planter and Bracket Systems.** Most garden centers and nurseries will stock some kind of planter and bracket system. The brackets are often track style and attach directly to your wall. The planter units hang from the tracks and can be moved around in any arrangement that suits you.

- **DIY Living Wall Units**. DIY living wall units are truly a mix of upcycled and reused products: old Mason jars, pallets, metal art pieces, planting cones or containers, bookshelves, and any other repurposed items. You are only limited by your imagination. These units are built with a creative eye and passionate heart by reusing an old item and transforming it into something new. Most DIY units are a soil-based concept, so they need the same maintenance as a traditional garden container might.

Wall Strength

Whether you make your own system or purchase a prebuilt or structured living wall system for your own special vertical garden, your most important consideration should be the structural integrity of the wall, fence, gate, or door that will support your vertical garden. Fences, for example, should be permanently installed with sturdy fence posts that are set in concrete to ensure that the fence will not tip from the heavy weight. Walls should be structurally sound and be able to withstand hundreds of waterings and other outdoor issues.

Most fences and exterior walls can easily support fifty to one hundred pounds of weight spread out over a 10-foot area. This does not mean that all walls can support the heavier weight of a soil-filled living wall. If you intend to install a large living wall installation, it is always a good idea to first consult a structural engineer to help you determine if the structure is adequate for the task.

Additional concerns for wall strength include watering techniques on the wall unit. If, for example, you have hose access and you regularly soak both the living wall system and wall with water from the hose, will it weaken the wall structure? If the fence or wall is built for outdoor conditions, then chances are it will be fine for system placement. Do not place a unit on plain drywall or any wall material that's weak and can rot or become further weakened by watering conditions. This will likely end in failure of the garden, wall, or both.

Dwight D. Eisenhower once said, "Plans are nothing, planning is everything." Indeed, this is particularly true with living wall structures and systems. Having a basic living wall system might seem to be a lovely idea and easy enough to assemble, but understanding the basic structure of the wall can help you plan a long-term living wall solution that is safe, beautiful, and long lasting.

Building your own living wall system by utilizing found objects or unusual planting containers can save you money and create opportunities for artistic ingenuity.

TOOLS THAT HELP

MOST TOOLS NEEDED FOR installation of the living walls included within this book are basic and simple to use. All living walls need to be hung evenly, so using a tape measure and a level for the initial wall placement is essential. Additional tools needed to install most of the units include a drill/driver for drilling holes and driving screws, a hammer, a pencil for marking the wall, and a ladder. Measure twice before drilling or hammering, as rehanging a vertical wall system is far more challenging than hanging it correctly the first time.

Living Wall Gardening Tools

In planting and designing the gardens, I discovered a few items that I consistently used when designing gardens that helped me plant and maintain the vertical wall gardens. These tools make it easier to work with living walls. See Resources, page 152.

- **A potting scoop** is a type of hand trowel that is designed specifically for working in small containers. They have a blunt tip, rather than the typical pointed tip, which minimizes spillage when you're transferring soil from a bag to the compact environment of a container. The high sidewalls also help reduce spillage. The blunt end makes it easier to scrape out last year's soil from the container too. A scoop isn't essential to living wall or container gardening, but I find them to be great time savers and they let me work cleaner.

- **Standard trowel**—When planting in very narrow areas, a standard trowel can work well. It is also good for digging out old plants for replacement. If you don't own a potting scoop, the standard trowel is the tool to use for many of your container gardening chores.

- **Weeder and cultivator**—Why would you need a weeding tool for a living wall? They have no weeds, right? Because a trim, hook-style cultivator enables a gardener to get into the wall planting container, pop a plant out, and replace it very easily. A traditional trowel does not do that effectively. Additionally, it makes planting seeds easier, as the sharp

↑ When building a living wall on a balcony or patio, you do not want soil spills to muddy up the area. Using a trowel that contains the soil well as you deliver it to the living wall system is a smart idea as it creates less mess for easy cleanup.

↑ While the CobraHead tool is mostly used for weeding in a traditional garden, I have found it remarkably helpful in digging trenches, hooking and pulling out old soil, and helping create space in living wall pockets. *Photo courtesy of the CobraHead Company*

Using pruners and scissors made from materials such as stainless steel enables you to trim and prune the living wall and not have them rust throughout the lifetime of the tool. Bold-colored handles prevent pruner loss, which can be inconvenient and even dangerous.

heads found on some weeding tools dig perfect rows in soil pockets.

- **Bypass pruner**—I use the bypass pruner to clean browning leaves and sticks off the living walls. Sometimes a little shaping of the plants on the wall with the pruner or even a small pair of scissors makes an enormous difference in cleanness and beauty. Over the years I've found that smaller cutting and trimming tools are very easy to misplace as they can slip into the weeds and hide easily. That's why I look for models that have brightly colored handles that make them easier to spot.

- **Rain wand**—A rain wand is a hose attachment that enables you to water one-handed while controlling the force of the water with your thumb. When you use a traditional garden hose without a rain wand, the force of the water stream can push the soil out of the living wall. By using a wand, the water comes out gently yet thoroughly waters all the various types of wall units. Definitely an important tool if you'll be using a garden hose to deliver water to your living wall.

- **Drinking-safe garden hose**—If you have access to a garden hose, it should be a drinking-safe water hose. Many garden hoses contain lead and other toxic ingredients. With this in mind, why would you water your organic garden with a hose that has the risk of toxic exposure? Use a drinking-safe garden hose for a healthier gardening experience.

Rain wands (also called watering wands) distribute water evenly and gently to your delicate living wall. Plug the watering wand into a drinking-safe hose for extra safety during the watering season.

↑ Row markers help with planting seeds and small seedlings in nice straight rows, which can have an impact on the success of your living wall design.

• **Row markers**—Depending on the living wall system you are using, you may or may not want to plant seeds. When you plant seeds, it can be important to make straight rows depending on your planting plan. Row markers help make straight lines. Simply place the row marker "dibber" in the soil on each side of your planting area and tie a string to them. Use the string as a guide to plant a straight line.

• **Seed storage unit**—They're not just for living wall gardens, but I've found that having a dedicated place to store your seeds is a very helpful resource for any gardener. I use a nifty little storage box I found online. It allows you to sort, categorize, and store the seeds so you do not lose them. This can be quite valuable, particularly if you are a part of a community garden where everyone needs to keep track of where they are and the specific expiration dates for the seeds.

• **Watering can**—My favorite watering can is an old metal one I found at a vintage thrift shop. What type of watering can is not critical, but you'll find enough choices out there that it's worth finding one you like. This is especially true if your living wall is located on an apartment balcony where you may not have a garden hose available. Make sure your watering can is small enough to fit easily under your water source and to lift overhead without spilling when watering a high hanging garden.

GETTING STARTED

GARDENING, WHETHER IT IS done in the ground, in a container, or on the wall, is a surprisingly rewarding experience. There is something beautiful and astounding that happens when you finally realize success with a plant. While most people assume that the astounding thing that happens is an emotional reaction based on pride, I say it is also the powerful connection that you have with a plant that you have nurtured and loved. Knowing that the plants you are growing are contributing to the health and welfare of your family and your community is also a powerful motivator to garden.

Living walls offer something particularly unique because of the striking visual effect produced by an upright wall. As we walk through our gardens, we spend much of our time looking down at the ground and noticing the paths, the plants, and the color. Yet raising your eyes upward can have a powerful effect from a design perspective. When you are faced with a medium-to-large wall installation, your entire body feels enveloped in the garden. It's like a hug from nature to sit next to a beautiful wall garden and absorb the sights and smells. Living walls help connect you with plants in a way that can only be described as immersion.

Sun Requirements

Once you have chosen the best system, you'll need to take into account the light conditions available in order to obtain plants that will thrive in your growing conditions. Each balcony, patio, or property has unique sun conditions. Choosing a site for a living wall means you must consider the sun in order to place plants in a successful location. Whether you are growing annuals, herbs, vegetables, or perennials, you must understand garden light exposure for the living wall. Typically, most balconies, fences, and entryways are in partial shade. Occasionally sun will hit these areas directly for most of the day, particularly if you have a southern exposure or no other buildings nearby. Full-sun plants need approximately six hours of direct sunlight per day. Part-sun plants will prefer filtered light during the day but still require four hours of sunlight per day. Shade plants can live with little or no sunlight, but they like indirect light or no light whatsoever. Watch the sun conditions on your site to determine the best plant for the specific sun and growing conditions you have.

By mixing shade plants with full sun plants, you might be creating a situation that will encourage failure. Try planting all the sun-loving plants in one living wall garden that receives a lot of direct sunlight throughout the day. Shade plants should be planted in a shady area, grouping the plants with similar light and watering requirements together in order to achieve success. Designing with light exposure in mind can save you a tremendous amount of money as well because you will have to water a living wall less if it is placed in the right position.

Chemical Use

There is absolutely no need to use heavy treatment chemicals with a living wall system. Many gardeners around the world reach for the chemical fertilizers, pesticides, fungicides, or herbicides first. In the United States, the home and garden market spends almost as much money—billions of dollars—on pesticides as the agricultural industry. Perhaps the reason for this is the "give me a pill" mentality of finding the quickest, easiest solution before finding the best and healthiest solution. Sometimes the healthier solution takes a few extra steps.

In the circle of chemical use, there is good news if you grow a vertical garden. Living walls do not need herbicides of any kind; in fact, they rarely have a weed to pull. When considering the use of pesticides, fungicides, or fertilizers,

Like all gardens, living walls start with active plants. They have a root system that needs to be cared for in order to grow and evolve into a larger plant.

Climate (and Microclimate)

Living walls can sometimes create warmer patches called microclimates. These areas form on walls that receive a south sun directly all day long; this heats up the wall, making a living wall a place where some plants can survive, even though they might not grow in the ground successfully. Additional considerations for living walls include an area's wind, humidity, and soil conditions. With good planning and a thorough knowledge of a plant's needs, one can purposefully create microclimates in order to expand the variety of plants you can grow in a season. Understanding plant zones and growth conditions can mean the difference between failure and success, particularly for vegetables.

go all-natural and organic whenever possible. When considering any application on a plant, be sure that you are treating the right thing. Pests, diseases, or improper planting could be the issue, and it is important for you to discover and treat the correct problem rather than use a random application and slam the plant with a solution that will not work.

Creating an environment within your vertical garden that builds a thriving and beautiful living wall starts with having the correct soil for the plants you are growing, then planting the right plant in the right location so that it receives the proper sunlight and environmental conditions to succeed. Your goal is to build a healthy community, not just a healthy living wall, and that success comes by creating a healthy foundation for the plant's roots to grow in.

WATERING THE LIVING WALL

THERE ARE SEVERAL OPTIONS for watering a living wall. While rainfall can have an influence on a living wall, particularly one that stands out a bit from the wall, such as a window box style of garden, you will be required to water the unit yourself and not depend on rainfall. Mostly, the best technique for watering your living wall is determined by which wall system you've chosen. Every two weeks, for instance, you should pull down the Sagewall system, which is the hydroponic system I used for the Hydroponic Pollinator Garden (see page 73) and soak it in water. Most all the other units need to be top- or front-watered, either with an automatic watering system or by hand, whenever they need it.

Planting your living wall units with plants that have similar watering requirements is as important as grouping plants based on sunlight requirements. Cactus and succulent plants need far less watering than other plants. Vegetables typically need to be watered more often. The rule of thumb is to water based upon the needs of the plants within the living wall unit. On average, let your living wall units dry out between watering just as you would a more traditional container garden. How often you are actually required to water is an individual living wall experience. Typically it is better to water your plants deeply two to three times per week rather than giving them shallow sips every day.

Garden-hose watering systems may contain toxic materials. A recent study in Michigan has shown that many garden hoses contain lead that exceeds the safety level for children. Garden hose water quality was also tested and shown to contained bisphenol A (BPA) and phthalates that were twenty times higher than safe drinking-water levels. Rain barrels can provide a fresher, less chemical-loaded source of water for your living walls. Another benefit of using rainwater is reducing the strain on storm water systems. Storm-water runoff is the leading type of residential nonpoint source pollution and is a large concern for those monitoring our earth's oceans and water systems. Water from your roof normally flows through gutter downspouts and becomes runoff, eventually washing onto paved surfaces collecting chemicals and oil from cars and funneling down storm drains. Storm-water systems around the world are overtaxed. Doing your small part can make a big difference for the environment.

Another important consideration when watering is making sure that you water at the right time of day. Watering your living wall in the morning before 10:00 a.m. or in the evening after 6:00 p.m. ensures that water stays in

Whether you hand water with a watering wand or use a special automated irrigation system (bottom photo), watering your living wall is key to its success.

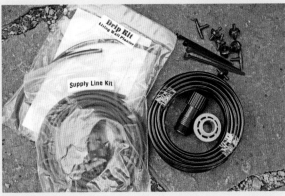

the soil for a longer period of time without drying out. Water at the base of the plants whenever possible, avoiding heavy leaf watering to prevent fungus and mildew issues.

SOIL AND COMPOST

WHETHER GARDENING IN THE ground, in a container, or in a living wall, getting nutritional material to a plant's root system is the secret to success. While some systems are hydroponic, the majority of the units discussed in this book require soil. Good soil is the most important ingredient in your living wall system, because if roots are healthy, then the stem and rest of the plant will also be healthy.

Because living walls are frequently raised up and exposed to wind and air, they will dry out faster than traditional container gardens, which can mean you have to water more. While growing the typical annuals, vegetables, and perennials, you will need a soil that is less airy and a bit heavier to help it have stronger water retention. You can increase the weight of your soil so that it will hold more water by mixing traditional potting soil with other natural ingredients or by making your own soil. These ingredients include compost and worm castings. Both have the added benefit of increasing complicated microbial growth within the soil around the roots. Yard clippings and food scraps make up one quarter of the United States' solid waste in landfills and produce methane, a greenhouse gas, as they decompose. Composting and making your own worm castings in a kitchen worm-casting bin will help the environment as well as your living wall. Do not add noncertified organic water crystals made from chemical polymers or artificial fertilizers to your soil mixes, and always grow with few or no chemicals whenever you can.

Making your own compost from leaves or kitchen waste is a terrific way to save money and contribute something amazing to a living wall root system. See pages 149 to 151 for more information on composting.

Homemade Soil Recipes

Several homemade soil mix combinations are compatible with the living wall gardens in this book. If you're using potting soil, choose an organic product brand that includes worm castings as part of the ingredient list. If you cannot find an organic soil with worm castings, add a cup or two of worm castings directly to your soil mix if you are able; it is a great way to retain moisture. Each of these recipes can be mixed in a large bucket or wheelbarrow. See Resources, page 152.

EASIEST STANDARD LIVING WALL SOIL MIX

1 part organic potting soil with worm castings
1 part organic rotted composted manure or plain compost
1 part course builder's sand

HOMEMADE STANDARD LIVING WALL SOIL MIX

2 parts compost
1 part presoaked coir peat
1 part vermiculite
1 to 2 cups worm castings

CACTUS AND SUCCULENT LIVING WALL SOIL MIX

1 part organic potting soil with worm castings
1 part perlite
1 part course builder's sand

EXTREMELY WATER RETENTIVE LIVING WALL SOIL MIX

(needs strong drainage)
1 part organic potting soil with worm castings
1 part organic rotted composted manure
1 part plain compost

↑ Using organic soil whenever possible ensures that what you grow will have an organic and all-natural foundation, especially important when growing vegetables and herbs or pollinator plants, for example.

↑ Adding the best soil mix to the living wall system will help the roots of the plants adapt and grow more readily, building a successful foundation for your plants.

↑ Worm castings for garden soil are easy to produce using a worm compost bin. You can also purchase bagged organic worm castings if you prefer. Mix worm castings into almost any soil mixture to increase moisture retention. See pages 149 to 151.

↑ Bloodmeal is a fine example of a natural fertilizer; it is filled with nitrogen and is good for most leafy plant's root systems. Follow directions on the package when using any fertilizer.

↑ To make your own compost tea, simply mix composted manure with water or soak compost tea bags. Add the tea to enrich the plants at watering time.

Natural Fertilizers

Living walls are essentially container gardens and, while organic fertilizer is not absolutely needed to grow a plant, the plant normally becomes stronger and more productive if fertilized organically and on a regular basis. Also, vegetables are more likely to need an organic fertilizer than other plants. When a slow-release fertilizer is added at planting time it has been proven that vegetables are more likely to succeed and produce more. For example, the University of Maryland did a research study on pepper production and doubled production by mixing slow-release fertilizer in at planting time. Vegetables can be lightly fertilized with an organic product every two to three weeks throughout the primary growing season. Compost tea can be added regularly at watering time.

One note, however: using any fertilizer when it is not necessary will not improve the condition of your plants and could simply cause a misbalance in the living wall system. Before you apply fertilizer, always ask the question, "Do I really need to add this?"

CHOOSING AND OBTAINING PLANTS FOR YOUR LIVING WALL

Choosing plants at the nursery can be a daunting experience. It helps if you build a suitable list of plants based on the growing conditions for your living wall.

WHAT TYPES OF PLANTS should you use in your living wall? That answer can best be determined once you understand the gardening conditions where you are growing.

What planting zone do you live in? How much light does the wall area where you'll be planting your living wall get? If it receives part-shade instead of sun, then it will be possible to plant vegetables, but you might want to consider the vegetables that perform better in shade.

Much like traditional gardens, living wall gardens in cooler planting zones should not be planted until after the last frost in the spring. It's important to research your local growing area to better understand when to plant, particularly if you are a new gardener. Consulting with a horticulturist at a nearby locally owned garden center or a college agricultural extension office can help you make wise plant selections.

Depending on your lifestyle and schedule, you may choose to purchase pregrown vegetables or bedding plants, houseplants, or perennials; or, you may prefer to grow your own from seed. When making purchases of these types of products, consider buying from local sources. When a bedding plant is grown locally you will be saving in "energy miles," which is the amount of energy expended in relationship to the production, storage, and delivery processes for products such as plants.

Another concern when purchasing plants from nurseries is neonicotinoids. They are a class of insecticides that are very similar to nicotine and have been known to show toxicity in mammals, birds, and insects. These chemicals have far-ranging and adverse effects on our ecology worldwide. Many good insects are being affected, including honey bees, which seem to be experiencing colony collapse disorder as a result of the neonicotinoid exposure. Ask local garden centers if they use neonicotinoids in the growing of their plants. If they do use the chemical, do not shop at that garden center and find one that uses fewer chemicals in their growing process. Think green, then buy local and chemical-free at every opportunity to save energy and pollinating insects and to do the right thing for the environment.

Plants from Seed

Why grow from seed? The most obvious answer to that question is that you cannot get some plant varieties in vegetative form. If you want to grow some heirloom types of vegetables, for instance, you will need to source those seeds from a seed company. Another wonderful benefit of growing your own plants from seed is that you can determine how much chemical exposure each plant gets.

Seed starting is quite easy and a great way to save money as well. Starting seeds can be done inside four to six weeks before planting or outside, sown directly into the soil. If starting your seeds inside, you need a sunny window or growing lights above the seedlings. Follow the specific directions on the package for seed treatment.

Use an organic commercial seed-starting soil mix that focuses on organic plant growth. There are dozens of seed-starting kits on the market that are easy to use. Moisten the soil mix, fill the potting cells, and place a single preprepared seed in each cell of a seed tray according to seed packet directions. Keep moist until germination, then water regularly. Use organic liquid fertilizer or compost tea to improve growth.

About two weeks to ten days before your official planting date, bring the trays of seedlings outside in a shady area that is out of direct, hot sunlight or drying wind. Protect from cold temperatures by moving in and out at night if

↑ Growing your own seedlings is a good way to save money and be more sustainable as it allows you to control if the seedlings are grown organically or not. Starting seeds is quite easy and a rewarding experience.

necessary, gradually exposing the seedlings to stronger outdoor conditions. Once the plants have hardened off, it is time to plant them in your living wall. It is important to wait until danger of frost has passed.

Growing Annuals and Tropical Houseplants

An annual is a plant that germinates from a seed, grows, flowers, and dies, experiencing its entire life cycle in one growing season. They are often the most colorful and florific flowers in the garden, which gives gardeners a sense of instant gratification. Many annuals flower all season long and have fascinating shades and textures. There are annual plants that are colorful, scented, and attractive to pollinators or beneficial wildlife. However, there are many annuals that seem to have no pollinator attraction, no scent, and no obvious benefit to the environment other than the nonstop blooms they bring to your garden.

Tropical houseplants are often used for living wall gardens because they offer extreme versatility in texture and foliage color, with many vining varieties. Because tropical houseplants do not overwinter outside well in most regions, it is best to treat the tropical houseplant as if it were an annual—only growing one life cycle in a season. It is easy to pop a houseplant out, repot it, and save it for next season's

Rootbound plants are plants that have an overgrown root system within their pots when purchased at the nursery or garden center. Bring the plants home and gently tease the roots loose so they will expand into the soil.

↑ Annuals can be both flowering varieties of plants or leafy plants. Many foliage annuals make a powerful color statement in the living wall garden.

living wall display if you would like to keep the houseplant love going year-round.

My garden has a significant display of annuals I consider dual-duty plants. Herbs such as oregano, cilantro, and globe basil help encourage bees, who love their scented flowers. Besides functioning simply as a beautifying tool in the garden, ornamental herb and vegetable edibles such as Swiss chard, kale, 'Bull's Blood' beets, and purple basil can help feed your community. Many annual flowers such as nasturtium, pansy, mint, snapdragon, and marigold are edible and make an astounding addition to a salad. Culinary uses for annuals are extensive, making a strong argument for having them in your garden. Every season I donate over 100 pounds of fresh ornamental edible vegetable and herb annuals to my local food pantry, and you can too.

Like vegetables, most annuals are very heavy feeders and can benefit from regular fertilization if you crave larger, more florific displays. Use an organic fertilizer recommended for flowering plants. Should you see fewer flowers and more foliage, you will know that you may be overfertilizing or might need stronger light exposure to see heavier flower production.

Planting an herb and vegetable living wall can help you grow more food in a much smaller space than in a traditional garden.

Growing Herbs and Vegetables

When I first began telling people about vegetable living walls, their opinion was that the gardens would be unattractive because vegetables are utilitarian and practical. Nothing could be further from the truth. Living walls are utterly astonishing when filled with vegetables. If planted correctly, you cannot tell they are traditional vegetables; the garden simply looks like a wall of beautiful garden color. Kale and cabbage have amazing blue shades in their leaves, and beets and Swiss chard can have an intense burgundy color.

Herbs, fruits, and vegetables can be perfect living wall ornamental edible plants, and they pair well with both annuals and perennials to bring a variety of colors to a vertical garden. Plant and fruit size matter when building a living wall. For instance, giant indeterminate tomatoes do not do as well in a living wall system as smaller herbs and vegetables such as beets, basil, and spinach. Because living walls frequently have a smaller planting area, kale, such as

'Redbor', which normally grows quite tall, can stay shorter and more dwarfed. Therefore, some larger leafy greens will do very well in a living wall as they are kept confined and do not typically overgrow.

Planting herbs and vegetables is easy; remove them from their cells or containers and gently tease apart the roots. Place them in the amended soil and cover their roots. Water thoroughly. Ornamental edibles are typically heavy feeders and have heavier watering requirements. With this in mind, it is beneficial to use the Extremely Water Retentive Living Wall Soil Mix formula (see page 33) as long as the planting system has excellent drainage. This mix helps retain water and also suggests rotted manure as an ingredient, which delivers a higher nitrogen content to the root systems. Adding an organic fertilizer made for vegetables at planting time and every several weeks will help kick up the vegetable production, particularly for leafy greens.

Growing Perennials

A perennial in a traditional bed such as a cottage garden or English perennial border is considered a long-term investment because the plant typically returns every year in the spring. Perennials can live for ten to twenty years and longer if cared for appropriately. They are easy to plant in a living wall; remove them from their cells or containers and gently tease apart the roots. Place them in the amended soil and cover their roots. Water thoroughly.

Perennials planted in a living wall might not live through an unusually harsh winter. With this in mind, you have two choices for perennial foliage: either pull the perennial out at the end of the season and replant it in fall in the ground to insulate the plant, replanting again in the spring, or leave it in the living wall and see if you get lucky and it overwinters into next season.

Perennials can be planted anytime, but they will see the most growth in a season if planted early in the spring. Understanding a perennial plant's growth habits, watering needs, and sun requirements is particularly important in the planting process so it will survive in the living wall. Planting the perennials with an organic fertilizer soil amendment will help its roots take hold.

There are several design techniques I use with perennial gardens, and these concepts can be applied to wall gardens as well. One design idea is to put all the tall perennials in the back, the medium height plants in the middle, and the short plants in the front. This works well with a living wall whether you are using perennials exclusively or mixing in annuals and vegetables—tall works best in back. When I plant an island perennial garden, I plant all the tall perennials in the middle of the bed, circled by medium height plants, with an outer ring of short plants. You can create this look with a living wall as well by planting the taller perennials in the middle area of the living wall, with the plants gradually receding in height on the sides. Much like hanging a picture on the wall, I focus on planting in odd numbers: one, three, five, seven, and so on. Odd numbers of plants look better grouped together whether they are in a living wall or in a garden bed. In the end, there are no hard and fast rules in design. Your imagination is the only limit on the design ideas you might use to build your little piece of living wall joy.

Ornamental Edible Herbs, Fruits, and Vegetables

A vertical wall system featuring colorful ornamental edible vegetables is smart: the design becomes more colorful and, at the same time, flashy-colored vegetables typically contain a higher level of nutrition and vitamin value. Here is a list filled with some of my favorite colorful foliage vegetables that are excellent in a living wall garden. If a type is not specified, it means that most varieties offer ornamental appeal:

- Anise Hyssop, 'Golden Jubilee'
- Arugula
- Basil, all purple varieties
- Basil, globe
- Basil, 'Pesto Perpetuo'
- Basil, 'Thai'
- Beet, 'Bull's Blood'
- Cabbage
- Celery
- Chives
- Collard greens
- Endive
- Fennel
- Kale, 'Dwarf Blue Curled'
- Kale, 'Italian Lacinato Nero Toscana'
- Kale, 'Redbor'
- Kale, 'Winterbore'
- Lavender
- Leaf lettuce
- Microgreens
- Mints
- Mustard greens
- Oregano, 'Amethyst Falls'
- Oregano, 'Variegated'
- Ornamental cabbage
- Ornamental kale
- Ornamental hot peppers
- Ornamental sweet potato vine
- Purple kohlrabi
- Radicchio
- Rosemary
- Rhubarb
- Silver thyme
- Spinach
- Strawberries
- Swiss chard
- Tarragon, Mexican
- Thyme, 'Golden Lemon'

PART II

LIVING WALL GARDENS WITH PURPOSE

IN THIS SECTION YOU will find twenty-one (well, twenty-three, really) complete designs for living walls you can build and grow in your own backyard. Each project includes a full list of the tools and materials you'll need, including a detailed plant list. Plus, you'll find tips, how-to instructions, and even a little trivia here and there. Whether you choose to make one of these designs exactly or to come up with your own unique plan, you'll discover that living walls help connect you with nature and plants in an immersion fashion, which leads to a greater sense of well-being. If you build a living wall that benefits your community, it will be an empowering experience.

Living wall gardening can be about environmental stewardship, community growth, feeding the hungry, therapeutic health, or simply adding enjoyment to your life. A living wall can provide a space in time for you to commune with nature for a quiet moment of peace. In my heart, I know that a garden of any kind is much more than "just a garden" because it is also a place that is beautiful and life-changing. Be a steward of nature; make a difference for yourself and others with a living wall garden.

- Herbal Cocktail Garden
- Moss and Shade Wall Art
- Vegetable "Balconies" Garden
- Fern Garden
- Cactus Living Wall
- Therapeutic Hanging Gardens
- Hydroponic Pollinator Garden
- Shade Pallet Garden
- Insulate-a-Wall Garden
- Bookshelf Fence Garden

- Succulent Living Wall
- Vertical Vegetable Farm
- Aphrodisiac Wall Garden
- Freestanding Entrance Garden
- Culinary Kitchen Garden
- Aromatherapy Garden
- Money-Saving Garden
- Smart Garden
- Colorful Living Wall
- Vitamin-Rich Culinary Garden
- Urban Water-Saving Garden

HERBAL COCKTAIL GARDEN

A Freestanding Herb Garden Planted with Mixology in Mind

ONE OF MY FAVORITE activities ever is to sit on my cocktail garden patio after a hard day of weeding, covered in mud and in my work boots, of course, enjoying a fine martini with my garden helpers and admiring the fruits of our hard work. You too can create a cocktail/entertaining living wall on a deck, balcony, or patio. Plant herbs that you can garnish or muddle or infuse, and you'll have a perfect place to promote home entertaining and community building. Plus, it just smells darned delicious. One truly amazing benefit of gardening with a living wall cocktail garden is no weeding. Therefore, you have my permission to skip the weeding and go straight to entertaining friends with to-die-for herbal martinis!

Herbal Sips and Muddling

Part of growing useful organic gardens is finding creative ways to use the bounty of the harvest. Herb and edible flower gardens are an easy way to grow foods that can enhance a beverage with a lot of flavor without adding a lot of artificial ingredients. Fundamentally, creating an herbal cocktail is not just for alcoholic beverage preparation. I like to call a refreshing herb-enhanced, non-alcoholic culinary treat an Herbal Sip. On a hot summer's day, there's nothing better than muddling strawberries and fresh mint together and pouring ice-cold lemonade over the top of the muddle for an astounding flavor burst.

Ice-cold water can be flavored in a similar way by muddling herbs, pouring the cold water over the herbs, and straining the mixture before drinking; the secret is in the muddle. A muddler is a wooden, plastic, or metal pestle that is an essential tool used in bartending. Use the fat side for mashing and muddling and the thinner side as a stirring tool. Simply put, muddling is a way of releasing the oils and flavors within herbs and fruits in order to provide a stronger flavor.

Infusing Flavor

Picking herbs and muddling them to enhance a cocktail's flavor is the easiest way to add flavor to a cocktail. You can kick it up a notch by macerating herbs, berries, or flowers in vodka, gin, or another liquor, infusing the flavors in a stronger, more condensed way. Infusing means to soak or steep an ingredient with a spirit in order to extract the dominant flavor of the item being infused. Vodka is frequently used as a part of the infusion process because it has a relatively neutral flavor that allows the infused herb flavor to stand out.

The infusing process is easy. Simply wash the herbs or flowers, shake excess moisture away, place in a Mason jar, muddle gently, and cover the ingredients completely with vodka or another spirit. Place the lid on the jar, lightly shake the container, and then store it out of direct sunlight for two to seven days. When the infusion is complete, strain the liquid into a clean jar and store it in the refrigerator or freezer.

Formula Box

Great-Tasting and Easy-to-Grow Cocktail Herbs and Edible Flowers

- Basil
- Cilantro
- Greek oregano
- Lemon thyme
- Lavender
- Mint
- Nasturtium
- Peony
- Peppermint
- Rose
- Rosemary
- Snapdragon
- Spearmint
- Violet

← When fresh herbs are within arm's reach, they are easy to use in culinary and cocktail delicacies.

↑ Mix edible sweet potato vines and flowers with herbs to create colorful, tasty ingredients and garnishes for drinks and food.

Stronger-flavored herbs and fruits take less time to infuse, while lighter flavors take longer. It's all about your taste preference. Better liquor creates a better infusion. Be sure, for instance, to use 80-proof alcohol or above, and preferably 100-proof.

Jellies

Extracting an edible herb's or flower's flavor can be super tasty; rose or lavender vodka infusions provide surprise flavors in cocktails. Another way to discover the flavor of an herb or flower is to convert the plant into a jelly. For example, peony jelly is created by pouring 5 cups of boiling water over one quart of peony petals and letting them steep overnight. Strain the liquid through cheesecloth in the morning, add the juice of one lemon and 3 cups of sugar, boil until the sugar is dissolved, then add 2 tablespoons powdered pectin, boil two minutes more, and pour in jars. The resultant pink jelly is marvelously fruity and can be used for many things—but is absolutely the best in a cocktail.

Making mint, lavender, or nasturtium jelly is a great way to incorporate a plant's essence into an herbal cocktail. Jelly cocktails are easy to make—muddle herbs first, add 2 tablespoons jelly, 2 or 3 ounces of liquor, and ice, then shake like crazy and strain into a martini glass. Absolutely delicious!

Growing and Harvesting

Herbs and edible flowers are a breeze to plant and maintain in a vertical wall system. Most herbs prefer full sun, but they can survive in partial sun or partial shade. Herbs and edible flowers are also uniquely beautiful, and having a living wall system jam-packed with herbs on your patio or balcony can be an overwhelmingly delicious scent experience. I once had a visitor come to my cocktail garden, sit next to the oregano, and exclaim, "It smells like pizza fresh out of the oven!"

Maintaining an herb living wall takes consistent watering and several applications of organic fertilizer throughout the season. Cilantro and other leafy herbs can bolt—that means to flower early—and grow less flavorful and leggy with fewer leaves. Trim browning plants back as well as any plants that might have bolted to keep your garden looking and smelling very fresh.

AN HERBAL COCKTAIL GARDEN

For this project, I used a manufactured window box system (see Resources, page 152). If you're handy, you can build something compatible pretty easily. This vertical planter can be fastened directly to a wall or used, with its feet, as a standalone system.

❶ Set up the freestanding living wall unit. It usually comes in two pieces that you secure with screws (provided).

❷ If you're attaching the unit to a fence or wall, your best bet is to let it rest just above the ground and simply drive a couple of deck screws through the top board and into the wall or fence. If you're hanging it so it is completely supported by the wall, use 3-inch exterior lag screws (with washers) driven through guide holes and into the wall—preferably at wall stud locations.

❸ If using as a standalone floor unit, simply hammer on the special blocks that function as the feet of the unit.

❹ Hang the wooden box frames onto the wooden back supports by hooking them on as shown in the manufacturer's directions.

❺ Turn over the plastic containers that line the boxes and punch out the drainage holes with a screwdriver.

❻ Mix container soil with organic fertilizer and fill soil in the unit (see page 33).

❼ Plant herbs and edible flowers tightly into the plastic garden containers, then drop the containers into the wooden frames.

❽ Water well.

↑ Punch holes in the bottoms of the containers, then fill the planting containers with a preferred soil mix.

↑ Plants used for this garden include globe basil, moss rose, oregano, purple basil, rosemary, sage, sweet potato vine, snapdragon, and thyme.

↑ Place soil-filled containers into the freestanding living wall unit.

← Once planted, water the unit regularly and trim off any dead leaves or branches. For cocktails and culinary dishes, simply snip up to one-third of the plant's leaves off. Let the plant grow back before harvesting again.

↑ Place containers of plants in your preferred design configuration. If satisfied with the design, dig holes with a trowel and place the plants within the living wall.

MOSS AND SHADE WALL ART

Low-Maintenance Moss Makes a Novel Design Statement in Any Home

GROWING MOSS AS A living wall first occurred to me when I journeyed to Ireland a few years ago. There, moss grows everywhere in abundance: on rocks, on walls, on animals, on homes, on absolutely everything. There was a certain magic about seeing mossy green patterns dancing along a rock fence wall that coaxed a passionate desire to touch. Some types of moss feel soft like lamb's wool, while other types feel prickly like a dry sponge. But all moss is magnificent in its beauty. I love moss, and surprisingly it makes rather wonderful living wall material.

Moss has been around for almost 300 million years and has been identified in ancient fossils. The moss family has more than 12,000 species of small spore-bearing plants ranging in size from microscopic forms to giant plants more than 40 inches long. They are typically distributed in freshwater areas of the world and do not tolerate salt water. Mosses are most commonly found in moist, shady locations and aid in soil-erosion control by providing a tight surface cover that absorbs water. Moss reproduces through spore production as well as by branching and fragmentation and regeneration from small pieces.

Which Moss Is Best for Living Walls?

While moss may grow abundantly in Ireland, and can easily grow everywhere in the northwest United States, it is not as easily cultivated in all locations. My garden now has moss, but I spent four years trying to grow moss and failing repeatedly. What I finally figured out is that I needed an expert to help me. I contacted David Spain from Mossandstonegardens.com. He gave me a quick overview on moss and how to grow it.

According to David, there are two primary types of moss used in gardening: acrocarpous and pleurocarpous. Each has unique characteristics. Pleurocarpous moss tends to form spreading carpets rather than erect tufts. They are freely branching plants growing in a more chaotic colonizing fashion. They can be fast growing and quickly regenerate when they are broken. Some pleurocarpous require heavy amounts of water and special care to get established. Acrocarpous mosses have a more upright growth habit. They tend to look "tufty" and are somewhat more tolerant of dry conditions. Their extensive branches create a more architectural mounded colony form. It is important to mark the difference between the varieties because acrocarpous's upright growth habit and drought tolerance makes it a better candidate for the conditions created by living walls.

Another benefit of acrocarpous moss is that it can survive without soil as long as it is an established plant and receives the water it requires. Dry moss is often found growing on rocks and other nonsoil locations. Lengthy contact with galvanized wire, zinc, and copper will kill this moss, so it is important that in living wall installations you do not let the moss touch galvanized products. Additionally,

Formula Box

Items That Can Be Converted into Creative Moss Living Wall Gardens

- Premade metal wall hangings
- Small photo frames
- Small embroidery hoops
- Found and recycled metal objects
- Metal wire baskets
- Old literature racks or brochure holders
- Flat tuna cans
- Glass cups
- Clay pots

← Dry moss can make a fabulous living wall if given the proper attention; it makes a lovely contribution to a shade garden or walkway and can fit in very narrow locations.

Dry moss (acrocarpous moss) is the best moss for use with this type of living wall as it is easier to maintain than moss that requires constant moisture or has other challenging growing requirements.

treated wood or chemicals can harm the moss, so it is better to grow organic and be aware of what touches the moss. If you find or create metal wall hangings for the dry moss, use nongalvanized material or paint over galvanized metal to block the moss-killing effect.

Wall Sculpture

Building a living wall using moss and wall sculptures, particularly metal art, is tremendously easy, and the wall art can be created from reclaimed materials or purchased as an already created art piece. Resale shops, garage sales, and online reseller stores have metal art in abundance and for reasonable prices. If you are concerned about protecting the wall on which you are hanging your living wall, the back of the art can be covered with a black hardware cloth or taken down for watering purposes and replaced once the moss has dried a bit. However, I used the art for a fence area and watered the wall sculpture directly.

Mosses do best in moderate temperatures and are evergreen plants through winter. They will thrive year-round as long as moisture and sunlight are available at the same time. Photosynthesis is possible even below 32 degrees Fahrenheit, so dormancy does not typically happen due to cold weather. Instead, most mosses go dormant because they are too dry. Typically, they return to active growth as soon as moisture fills their tissue. Although it's not necessary, if you want to bring the wall hanging inside during winter, simply water it in the shower when necessary, let dry, and then rehang inside. Bring it out again in the spring.

Finding moss is easy. While some garden centers sell moss, suppliers are easy to locate online. A soilless living wall requires minimal attention once established and is an incredible conversation piece in your garden and home.

A MOSS AND SHADE ART GARDEN

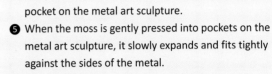

❶ Once your acrocarpous moss arrives, you will want to stretch the moss out in a shady area.

❷ If you cannot plant immediately, water the plants. Moss should be dry before fragmenting, so on the day you will be building your living wall, make sure the moss is very dry.

❸ To get the acrocarpous moss to stay in the wall sculpture unassisted, simply pull off a large piece of moss from the sheet of moss that arrived from the nursery.

❹ Take the large piece of moss in both hands, then compress and squeeze it tightly until it can fit into a pocket on the metal art sculpture.

❺ When the moss is gently pressed into pockets on the metal art sculpture, it slowly expands and fits tightly against the sides of the metal.

❻ Repeat until your art sculpture is filled as you like it.

❼ Hang the wall unit using a hammer and nails or deck screws.

❽ Water using the water recommendations on page 48.

↑ Begin with an item that can be stuffed full of moss. Upcycling or converting old items into a moss garden is an excellent idea. Paint any galvanized metal surfaces as the moss can be killed by prolonged exposure to them.

↑ Squeeze the moss firmly together until it is squished in a tight formation.

↑ Stuff the tight moss formation into pockets on the item you are utilizing for the living wall. Make sure that the moss is tight so it cannot fall out of the planting pockets.

↑ Water daily for the first month and follow the instructions listed on page 48 for specific watering requirements over a long period of time.

VEGETABLE "BALCONIES" GARDEN

These Hanging Veggie Boxes Deliver Fresh Food and Fresh Air

NUTRITION AND QUALITY AIR are two of the most important drivers of good overall health. Build this garden and install it next to an outdoor living area or near a window, and you'll be getting a good dose of both elements. Living wall gardens, full of plants that breathe in carbon dioxide and breathe out oxygen, are a fantastic way to help filter the air surrounding a living area. This oxygen reaches a city dweller with a living wall if he or she is sitting on the balcony or sitting inside the home with the window open. Having a view of the vertical wall garden from the interior of the home will both reduce stress and increase the green view. Most importantly, growing vegetables in the garden means that you will also be providing nutritionally sound food for you and your family, so the living wall provides extensive benefits beyond simple beauty.

As a young woman fresh out of school, I moved to the big city and lived in the downtown Chicago area. My neighborhood was filled with busy urban apartment dwellers, few parks, very little grass, and lots of noise and pollution. After only a few years away from the country and more natural environments, my health and allergies began to suffer. Not only did I miss the outdoors, but I craved green. I feel that by connecting myself to gardening again in later years, I was able to rescue my health.

Air pollution found in urban areas can cause long-term and short-term health effects. The elderly and young children are particularly affected by air pollution. Short-term health issues include sinus and throat irritation, allergy problems, and upper respiratory complications. Long-term health concerns are significantly more serious and can include lung cancer, respiratory and pulmonary disease, and brain, kidney, and liver damage.

Improving Mental and Physical Health

Because urban environments are filled with noise, traffic, and air pollution, they have a profound effect on us, both mentally and physically. Living without green can hinder our emotional development and increase levels of violence within humans. According to a study done at the University of Illinois Urbana-Champaign's Landscape and Human Health Laboratory, familial violence can be reduced if there is a view of landscaping or nature outside the windows of your home and workplace. This makes living walls a smart tool to use in living situations of all sorts. Whether in suburban or city living, improving air quality and the view outside our windows is critical. Living walls provide a substantial connection to nature that helps ease the effect of the modern concrete jungle. Additionally, green walls are known to mitigate the urban heat island effect by breaking up the concrete and flat surfaces.

Large Leaves Equal More Oxygen

When planning a vegetable balcony garden with air filtration and oxygen generation in mind, the question becomes, "How do I increase the oxygen levels with

Formula Box

Vegetables and Herbs That Make Great Oxygenators

- Arugula
- Basil
- Cabbage
- Collard greens
- Kale
- Lettuce
- Mint
- Spinach
- Swiss chard

← Improving air quality and providing food for your family is possible in an urban area by planting your own vertical balcony wall garden.

↑ Plants for this project include 'Bull's Blood' beets, collard greens, globe basil, kale, oregano, purple basil, and rosemary.

Tools needed

- 1 window box living wall system—purchased or built
- Allen wrench
- Hammer
- Screwdriver
- Containers
- Container soil
- Organic fertilizer
- Vegetables and herbs

If hanging on wall:

- Drill
- Exterior lag screws and washers
- Socket wrench
- Tape measure
- Level

the garden in order to bring more oxygen to my balcony or outdoor living environment?" We know that oxygen is respired by plant leaves. Each leaf produces an hourly output of about 5 milliliters of oxygen, with larger leaves producing even more. Plants with a larger concentration of leaves will produce more oxygen. Therefore, using leafy herbs and vegetables in a living wall garden serves a greater purpose than simply providing food: the plants will help increase oxygen levels near the garden.

All varieties of leafy houseplants make great oxygenators. There are many leafy green vegetables that are excellent for increasing oxygen output, such as Swiss chard, kale, lettuce, spinach, dandelion, watercress, arugula, bok choy, cabbage, and sorrel. Other excellent greens include collard, turnip, mustard, and beet greens. Oxygenating herbs include basil, mint, cilantro, parsley, and oregano. While the leafy vegetables are often larger than the herbs and therefore more likely to produce more oxygen, the herbs have unique scents that bring olfactory enjoyment to those sitting near the garden.

Sometimes apartment management or townhome associations do not allow drilling into balcony walls due to aesthetic concerns and potential long-term damage issues to the property. This situation can be easily remedied by using a portable or self-supporting vertical wall system that enables the living wall to stand completely on its own without a need to be attached directly to a wall, balcony, or fence.

Standalone Living Walls

Standalone vertical wall systems are easy to put together and offer the additional benefit of being movable should you need to relocate the garden. Another benefit of a portable garden is being able to maintain a garden while moving frequently. Jobs around the world often force workers to relocate several times a season. These same workers feel challenged in planting a garden. Why plant a garden if you will be moving to another city in just a few months? Conceptually, the standalone vertical wall system can be easily relocated, making it a positive option for workers who are more transient throughout the year. Best yet, this same vertical wall garden can produce a significant quantity of food in less than a 2-square-foot area of planting space. Portable gardens can provide the amazing health benefits of an oxygenation garden while providing organic vegetables to support better health.

Most leafy herbs and vegetables prefer at least a half day of sun but can survive with less light or high amounts of reflective light. To get the maximum oxygen benefit, the living wall should be placed just outside of the home or balcony entrance to treat visitors near the open door with waves of fresh-smelling air. Scented herbs are a fantastic addition as their fresh scent is stimulating. Portable living walls can also function as a beautiful place to rest the eye in an industrial area or a parking lot.

HOW TO BUILD

A VEGETABLE BALCONY GARDEN

Freestanding window box systems can be fastened directly to the wall or used as a standalone system that stands without being firmly attached. Either way works for growing most air-filtration plants.

1 Assemble or build a freestanding window box living wall system.

2 If you're attaching the unit to a fence or wall, your best bet is to let it rest just above the ground and simply drive a couple of deck screws through the top board and into the wall or fence. If you're hanging it so it is completely supported by the wall, use 3-inch exterior lag screws (with washers) driven through guide holes and into the wall—preferably at wall stud locations.

3 If using as a standalone floor unit, simply hammer on the special blocks that function as the feet of the unit.

4 Hang the wooden box frames onto the wood back supports by hooking them on as shown in the manufacturer's directions.

5 Turn over the plastic containers that line the boxes and punch out the drainage holes with a screwdriver.

6 Mix container soil with organic fertilizer and fill soil in the unit (see page 33).

7 Plant herbs and edible flowers tightly into the plastic garden containers, then drop the containers into the wooden frames.

8 Water well.

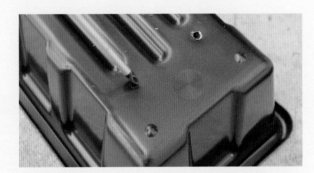

↑ Punch out the holes at the bottom of the plastic box liners.

↑ We designed and assembled the this urban living wall back at my garden, then relocated it to downtown Chicago. These window box–style living walls are very easy to transport. Here, the soil containers are filled before planting.

→ Creating a design and laying it out before you actually plant prevents mistakes and allows you to see symmetry in the design. Once you're satisfied with the design layout, plant the herbs and vegetables in the living wall system.

FERN GARDEN

A Stunning Vertical Wall Solution for Shady and Damp Locations

FERNS HAVE ALWAYS FASCINATED me; I love their green, airy, delicate limbs that wave in the breeze. As a little girl growing up on a farm, I rarely saw ferns growing unless I happened upon a stand of native ferns in the local woods. Farmers' wives would sometime hang Boston ferns from containers on their wide wraparound porches in the humid summers or perhaps grow Ostrich or Japanese ferns as in-ground perennials when a particularly challenging wet and shady spot presented itself. I have had great success growing ferns outdoors in recent years by placing them in an area that is best suited for their special growing requirements.

Growing ferns as a living wall is an excellent idea for unique circumstances: ferns are definitely built for indirect light and moisture. They will need to have a regular and consistent source of water and humidity and prefer an air humidity around 50 percent. More critically, ferns are the perfect living wall garden solution for an extremely damp, humid, and partially shady area. Do you have a wall that continually grows green moss? This would be the spot to build a living wall garden made entirely from ferns. A whole wall of plants is another way to protect an exterior siding or brick from greening up because of moss. It also provides an extra layer of insulation on your home during the hot summer months. Studies have demonstrated that having a green wall on an exterior surface of your home can make that wall up to 50 degrees cooler than an exposed wall. This means that less heat is radiated inward to the interior of your home.

Perennial Ferns

While there are thousands of types of perennial ferns, these plants typically require an in-ground planting to overwinter in most areas around the nation. Therefore, it is best to treat this exterior wall garden as an annual planting rather than expect it to be a year-round exhibit. Most ferns are known as shade plants, but all ferns seem to be more prolific when grown in partial shade that offers a lot of indirect light.

Several types of perennial fern selections can be used on the wall. Many varieties offer a colorful and attractive solution; ghost fern has white tones mixed in with green and gray, autumn fern turns a fall orange color late summer, and Japanese painted fern has a rainbow of tones ranging from black to mauve. Mixing these with the greener deer, maiden hair, or ostrich ferns would definitely create an interesting look on a home's wall. There are dozens of other varieties that have unique shapes and curious leaf patterns. The problem with selecting perennial ferns is that they are relatively slow growers and rarely form fully developed stems or leaves the first year of growth. Unless you purchase a more expensive, fully grown perennial, the wall will look rather barren until the plants

Formula Box

Soil Medium for a Fern Wall Garden

- 1 part organic potting soil
- 1 part rotted manure
- 1 part sand or perlite
- 1 part shredded sphagnum

Tip

Before planting your annual ferns, groom them. This means to clean up dead or browned fronds and clip back any problematic growth. Regularly grooming throughout the season is required to keep the plants looking their best on your living wall.

← A fern wall provides additional insulation and complements garden landscaping.

↑ Boston ferns fill in fast and make an impressive structure, but they are not hardy and need to overwinter indoors in most areas.

develop more fully. To overwinter perennial ferns, you need to bury their roots in the ground well before the first frost, then pull them out again in the spring.

Annual Ferns

To have an immediate and full fern display, purchase a fully grown Boston fern or similar variety, which is primarily known as a houseplant. Boston fern, sword fern, or petticoat fern are all varieties with the same basic growing requirements. It is easy to achieve success with these ferns planted outdoors in indirect light during the humid seasons. Ferns such as these can be found growing wild in Florida and other subtropical and tropical zones around the world and truly prefer warm tropical conditions whenever possible. The humid days of summer throughout most of the country provide excellent conditions for this houseplant. Boston ferns and similar varieties prefer temperatures in the 75- to 80-degree range and can survive nights down to 55 degrees.

Soil, Water, and Fertilizer

Soil requirements for ferns are specific. Most ferns prefer their roots in a well-draining mix rich in nitrogen. Mix 1 part organic potting soil, 1 part rotted manure, 1 part sand or perlite, and 1 part shredded sphagnum for a healthy growing medium. This soil mixture provides nutrients and enhances proper moisture requirements but still allows for good drainage.

Providing the proper water and feeding for your ferns is important. Using tepid rainwater from rain barrels is best because it provides a mostly chemical-free solution for the plants. Keep the soil consistently moist; do not let it dry out completely. If the plant becomes too dry, it will begin to look dull and lifeless and eventually brown out. Apply a nitrogen-rich organic plant food once per month from April to September. Fish emulsion gives excellent results; natural and organic fertilizers are preferred.

Overwintering Ferns

There is an additional benefit in choosing the Boston fern: at the end of the season, you can bring the plants indoors to use as houseplants. After winter has passed, you can place the ferns back out for use as a living wall again. Boston ferns sometimes have an adjustment period when moved inside. If the leaves are shedding and browning, it needs a little help to overcome the drier, cooler, dimmer conditions it might be encountering indoors. Homes in the winter are often at a local humidity level around 10 to 15 percent. Try moving the plant to a bright west-facing window to help it get a bit more indirect light, and mist it daily with a mister throughout the winter season. If at all possible, do not place the houseplant over a heating duct as too hot conditions can sometimes cause fungus to grow. Do not feed the plant during the winter months; it will snap back in the spring once it is taken outside again and its summer regimen is reinstituted. If overwintered with the proper attention, it can easily be hung outside again in spring with little complication.

A FERN GARDEN

1. Hang cone wall planters, evenly spaced, in your preferred pattern. Measure carefully, drill guide holes, and then attach zip ties to the cones. Fasten the zip ties to the wall with exterior screws, such as deck screws. Hooks with screws can also be used to secure the planters.
2. Fill cones with the soil mix recommended for ferns (see page 56) using the trowel.
3. Measure an appropriate amount of organic fertilizer into the soil; mix well.
4. Plant ferns individually in each living wall cone.
5. Water well.

↑ Hang the planters and double-check that they are spaced evenly.

↑ Measure and space the planting cones carefully.

↑ Snip drainage holes in the bottom of each planting container.

↑ Water the ferns regularly with a watering wand or a watering can.

Cactus varieties planted in this living wall unit include Argentine opuntia, Peruvian old lady cactus, Eve's needle crest, grafted cactus, golden ball cactus, ming thing cactus, chamaelobivia hybrid cactus, hamatocactus hamatacanthus, and echinopsis purpureopilosa cactus.

Tools Needed

- 1 bracket-hung framed art wall—purchased or built (see Resources, page 152)
- Screwdriver or drill/driver
- Exterior screws
- Tape measure
- Level
- Cactus soil mix
- Organic fertilizer
- Cactus
- Trowel
- Tong with wrapped tips and/or gloves
- Gravel or moss (optional)

choose to plant is up to you—straw flowers or without, bold colors, spiky, flat, hairy, rounded, or short—but no matter which variety, the cactus is a delightfully easy plant to have in a living wall garden.

Edible Cactus

There are a few varieties of cactus that are edible and could easily be included in a living wall garden. Opuntia or prickly pear cactus is a paddled cactus used in Southwestern and Mexican cooking. To consume this variety of cactus, one must first de-spine the plant, then boil it in water until tender. It is excellent in soups, stews, and served in a burrito, taco, or even *huevos rancheros* with spice and other vegetables added. Opuntia's unusual paddle shape and growth habit make it an excellent feature plant that provides an additional useful purpose for your living wall—edibility.

To grow a healthy cactus plant, one must first purchase a plant that is healthy. Avoid plants that have cuts or bruises, damaged spines, or uneven growth. Some plants appear to have put in newer growth that looks sprawling or spindly due to dimly lit store growing conditions—avoid these plants as they will remain disfigured permanently. Purchase a plant that looks strong, with good color and shape.

While cactus might be surprisingly simple to manage, they are prickly and can be difficult to plant. Handle the cactus very carefully and wear tough gloves so that you can prevent prickles and spines from piercing your skin. Wrap the end of cooking tongs with duct tape, so the metal does not cut into the cactus skin, and use the tongs for lifting and placement. Should you get pricked with the cactus needles, use tweezers to gently pluck the spines out of your skin.

Growing Requirements

Most cactus varieties have similar growing requirements. They all require excellent drainage. To encourage good drainage, plant your cactus garden in a purchased cactus soil mix or make your own growing medium, using 1 part potting soil, 1 part perlite, and 1 part coarse builder's sand.

Although they need far less water than ferns or other heavy drinkers, cactus still needs to be watered regularly. Normally, more water is required during the new growth period that happens in late winter or early spring due to higher light growth. A light dousing once per week for small plants and every two weeks to a month for larger, well-established plants will do. When temperatures rise in later summer, growth will slow down and the cactus will require far less water.

Cactus need warmth and bright light, but full sun is not always the proper choice. Plant the varieties that prefer the same sunshine levels together. When temperatures drop below 50 degrees at night, consider moving the living wall to an interior location and protecting it through the winter. Place in front of a window with strong light exposure.

↓ Cactus garden living wall components that will help with planting include a framed art wall, cactus, trowel, gloves, tongs, and gravel or moss (optional).

A CACTUS LIVING WALL

❶ Measure carefully, and then hang the framed art wall unit using exterior-rated screws or other fasteners if listed in the manufacturer's directions.

❷ Lay the system flat and use a trowel to fill it with cactus soil mix.

❸ Measure an appropriate amount of organic fertilizer into the soil; mix well.

❹ Arrange cactus in the container.

❺ Plant cactus carefully into the soil, using tongs and special gloves to prevent injury.

❻ Water well while the unit is still lying flat.

❼ While the water is draining, attach the mounting bracket to a secure vertical wall, keeping the brackets level and spaced properly.

❽ Hold the planted unit and frame together by placing one hand on the back side of the planter and the other hand on the underside of the frame. The collector tray piece should be at the bottom. Carefully place the planter onto the bracket.

❾ If the framed unit you are using has a water delivery system, install the irrigator and the collection tray as directed by the manufacturer.

❿ When watering in the future, water through the top irrigator unit.

↑ Cactus plants can be quite prickly, so protection is absolutely necessary when planting the living wall. Use rose gloves or another heavy glove to prevent injury.

↑ Soil requirements for cactus and succulents are different than for traditional living walls. Use the appropriate mix when filling the living wall pockets.

↑ Carefully level the hanging bracket so the garden will hang straight.

↑ Secure the hanging bracket with a screwdriver once you are satisfied with the positioning.

↑ Once planted, hook the framed art wall unit onto the bracket.

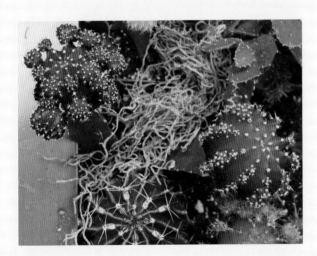

↑ Should you prefer the soil to be hidden, gently press gravel or moss into the base of the plants.

→ Use soil to secure the cactus roots inside the planting pockets so that the plants will hang tightly without falling out.

THERAPEUTIC HANGING GARDENS

Two Simple Living Wall Arrangements that Turn a Plain Gate into a Calming Garden Element

CONNECTING WITH NATURE IS powerful. There have been times in my life when I have walked into a garden and felt better because I've connected with the environment in a personal and deeply emotional way. Sitting on a park bench inhaling the smell of flowers in springtime or enjoying a pond that sits in quiet solitude can spark memories, facilitate meditation, or build a bond with the outdoors. Being in nature is healing in its own right, but imagine if your health, both mental and physical, could be improved simply by making a living wall garden. Or two! In this project you'll see a pair of creative gardens designed to unleash the restorative power of plants. We hung ours from a wood garden gate, but they can be mounted on any vertical surface.

Healing Garden Design

Home gardening has long been viewed as an essential leisure activity, not just simple maintenance and labor. Yet hard science supports the conclusion that the human psyche's exposure to nature through gardening helps heal the body and the spirit. Knowledge of the therapeutic landscape came into the broader public's awareness when Wilbert Gesler introduced the terminology in his book *The Cultural Geography of Health Care*. Originally, the definition Gesler proposed was that landscapes were places with "an enduring reputation for achieving physical, mental, and spiritual healing" and could become a critical element in healing and health care conveyance.

Since Gesler's original theory was introduced, therapeutic gardens have become established as a distinct garden design category, often including an artistic or beauty-centered element. Therapeutic gardens are built for their restorative benefits and might be considered healing, meditative, or calming. However, it could also be a garden that is designed to stimulate energy or encourage memory. Each therapeutic garden is created with a healing purpose in mind that will help visitors feel both emotionally and physically better.

Therapeutic gardens are not defined by specific structural parameters, but they can generally help patients become more healthful and well by creating an atmosphere where a person can explore his or her emotional health. Healing parks or gardens are often seen at hospitals and health centers to help encourage this type of exploration. Size is not a concern. A special living wall can be built to fit one's home balcony and designed with positive healing energy in mind. The wall can give a homeowner or apartment dweller immediate access to fresh scents and beauty that might stimulate introspective thought and meditative relaxation. Building a healing garden can be a simple task that helps care for a person's medical and emotional needs.

Formula Box

Scented Herbs That Stimulate Healing

- Basil
- Basil, globe
- Lemon thyme
- Mint
- Oregano
- Rosemary
- Thyme

← Scents from the therapeutic herbs waft by every time the gate is opened and closed. Hanging a Mason jar living wall on a gate might seem precarious, yet the jars are quite secure and allow the gate to open and close with ease. You can also choose another vessel, such as fabric planting pockets (inset).

Therapeutic gardens employ both color and scent to achieve their goals. A few plants you might find in them are oregano, rosemary, and creeping jenny.

Calming Therapy

Healing living walls, in their simplest form, can be contemplation gardens that provide an area of quiet where one might consider one's spirituality, religion, or peaceful feelings. This calm and safe environment can help reduce agitation or stress as well as increase the ability to focus so that healthful recovery is more achievable. Restoring one's emotional balance in life, particularly when an individual might be in the middle of illness and invasive medical treatments, can help mitigate the extreme stress that hospitals and institutionalized environments can stimulate during medical treatments.

While a healing garden should generally be calming and beautiful, it should also focus on the specific requirements of the person who is in need of the healing area.

For instance, if someone needs more exercise or to improve strength and balance, the vertical wall garden could be placed on a fence or wall at the end of a long alley or lawn that is a distance from a home's entrance. This creates a destination to walk to and strengthens muscles. Additionally, scents are known to stimulate mental awareness. Planting a living wall with flowers and herbs with a noticeable fragrance could be critical to a stimulating environment. Perhaps a healing living wall could be placed in a shared courtyard for many to enjoy. Living walls on gates are also a great possibility, as entering an alley, home, or garden can be more welcoming if scents and beauty greet arriving visitors.

Design Notes

In order to determine what plants should go into a healing garden, it is important to first know what might help the people who will be visiting the garden. To be most effective, your garden design should be based on conversations with or knowledge of the unique needs of the primary garden users. Will it be best for the users to have a stimulating garden or a calming garden? Should there be an activity associated with the garden, or is it simply a quiet, meditative area? Although the therapeutic garden may be custom-designed for one specific person, hanging a scented healing garden in an entry or door area will inspire fresh, healing scents for anyone who walks through gates and brushes by the wall garden.

Therapeutic living walls can be large, small, or anywhere in between. It depends on the space available and the specific therapeutic needs. Using upcycled Mason jars as the crafty soil base for the living wall plantings enables a living wall gate that is part art installation and part garden—built for its fragrance, beauty, and calming effect for any who happen by.

A THERAPEUTIC MASON JAR GARDEN

❶ Carefully drill a drainage hole in the bottom of each canning jar using a ceramic tile and glass bit. Please see the safety tip ("Drilling Holes in Glass," below) first.

❷ Measure an appropriate amount of organic fertilizer into the soil; mix well.

❸ Fill the jars with planting soil.

❹ Plant scented herbs and flowers in the jars.

❺ Water well.

❻ Cut a 4-foot length of wire or twine.

❼ Tie a length of wire or marine-rated cord around the top of each canning jar, just below the threads at the top, to form a loop for hanging the jar. Vary the lengths of the loops if you're hanging the jars from the same support (like the gate pickets I hung them on).

❽ Hang the jars so they are far enough a part not to bump into each other if they swing around when the gate opens and closes.

Tools Needed

- 5 to 7 Mason jars
- Drill/driver
- ½-inch ceramic tile and glass bit
- Duct tape
- Exterior screws
- Tape measure
- Level
- Wire or marine-rated cord
- Container soil
- Organic fertilizer
- Herb plants
- Trowel or spoon

↑ Mason jars of any kind or style can be used, although the standard one-quart size works well for this project. If you can find colored ones, go for it.

Drilling Holes in Glass

Planting containers need to drain, but Mason jars are designed to be watertight. To allow for drainage, you'll need to drill a drainage hole in the bottom of the jar. Although it might sound a little scary, there is no need to worry—you can do it yourself. With the right tools and techniques, it's simple and safe. You'll need a special drill bit called a ceramic tile and glass bit. They have a spear-shaped tip, and a ½-inch one is reasonably priced. Wearing a good heavy glove and eye protection, hold the jar securely on a soft surface, such as the ground. Put a piece of duct tape over the bottom of the jar to help keep the glass from flaking or splintering, and drill right through the tape and glass together. Use slow drilling speed and don't push down hard, especially as you're nearing the end of the cut. Remove the tape and dispose of the glass dust immediately.

Herbs included in this therapeutic Mason jar living gate are sage, rosemary, and thyme.

↑ Use an organic, moisture-retentive soil mix to help the plants hold and retain moisture in a tight-rooted growing situation.

↑ Plant the Mason jars using a spoon to help backfill the soil within the container.

↑ Once planted, the jars should be tied with wire or marine cord that won't rot and hung on the wall or gate.

A THERAPEUTIC FABRIC POCKET GARDEN

- 4 to 6 planting pockets (see Resources, page 152)
- Large black jack chain, ⅝-inch link (length is determined by measurement)
- Threaded rods, ⅜-inch
- Wing nuts, ⅜-inch
- Standard nuts, ⅜ inch
- Tape measure
- Hack saw
- Wire cutter
- Pliers
- Spray paint (optional)
- Container soil
- Organic fertilizer
- Herb and decorative plants
- Trowel or spoon

1. Measure the height of gate, door, or wall area to confirm length of chain needed.
2. Measure the threaded rods and cut them at an even length so that each rod can be threaded through the planting pockets' fastening hole on the sides of the wally to act as a support.
3. (Optional) Place the cut rods, wing nuts, and standard nuts on a flat, protected surface and paint. Let dry.
4. Lay out the pockets on the ground one on top of the other, making sure the pockets fit within the area they'll hang.
5. Screw standard nuts onto the threaded rods, screwing down about 1½ inches.
6. Lay the black jack chain around the edge of the pockets on the ground, giving extra chain at the top in order to use it as the hanging area.
7. Use the wire cutters to cut the extra chain off at the bottom of the display.
8. Measure the area between the fastening holes so that all the sides are even.
9. Starting at the bottom of the chain, gently pry open the chain with the pliers and place the rod with the nut to the inside of the chain.
10. Recrimp with the pliers to close the chain link.
11. Screw the wing nut on the rod to the outside of the chain.
12. Tighten gently.
13. Touch up spray paint (optional).
14. Repeat the process for each side of every pocket, making sure nuts are evenly placed so that they hang evenly.
15. Hang the planting pocket unit on fence or gate, dropping the chain around the top of the fence to act as a support.
16. Measure an appropriate amount of organic fertilizer into a bucket of soil; mix well.
17. Fill each pocket with planting soil.
18. Plant scented herbs and flowers in the pockets.
19. Water well.
20. Move the mobile garden as needed or keep it in a permanent location.

→ Supplies for making a portable therapeutic fabric pocket garden include felt planting pockets, black chain, rods, nuts, and bolts.

↑ Measure the width of the pockets. Then, using a hacksaw, cut the threaded rods to that length.

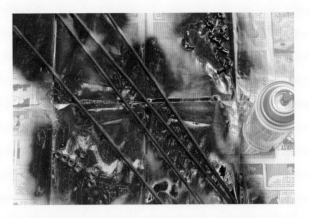

↑ Spray-paint all metal parts to match the color of the chain.

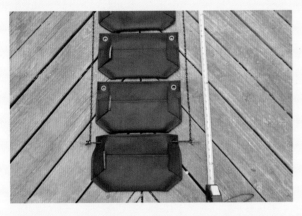

↑ Once all pieces are gathered together, lay out the pattern for hanging, measuring carefully.

↑ Once it is determined where the rods should reside on the length of the chain, snip one of the chains and wrap it carefully around the rod. Use nuts and bolts to hold the rod in place.

↑ After the rods are assembled, test the hanging system to make sure it fits well on the location you have in mind.

↑ Because the pockets are small, it might be necessary to press the roots flat before planting in the soil mix. Backfill between plants with soil as needed.

HYDROPONIC POLLINATOR GARDEN

This Beautiful (and Soilless) Flowering Garden Offers Food and Shelter for Bees and Butterflies

THIS COMPACT FLOWERING GARDEN is so gorgeous that it almost makes you forget what it is for. Right now, we are living in a pollinator crisis. Ten years ago, my gardens were filled with hundreds of bees and butterflies flying, landing, and pollinating, truly making a difference for the flowers and vegetables on my property. Now when I am out working in my garden, I only see a few pollinators doing their thing, and my heart is aching over it. Gardeners and farmers around the world have started sharing their concerns about our pollinators, and the results have been staggering. Bees are particularly important to humanity as they pollinate one-third of the world's food supply, a large percentage of medicinal plants, and 90 percent of the world's wild plants. Currently, more than $15 billion annually in American food crops are pollinated by bees. Without bees, humankind will suffer a devastating drop in the food supply and a domino effect of massive economic disaster. If you are not concerned about this situation, you should be. We need more pollinator gardens, and a living wall garden is a great start.

There are many types of pollinators besides bees. For instance, beetles pollinate magnolia trees. A small fly pollinates most of the cacao plants that supply the world's chocolate. Pollinators are animals that cause plants to make seeds and fruits. Most pollinators do this by relocating pollen from one part of a flowering plant to another part, causing fertilization. Only fertilized plants can create fruit or seeds. Without the fertilization process, there would be no plants because they would not be able to reproduce and, of course, there would be no fruit or seeds. While bees are the most prominent workers, there are also butterflies, beetles, flies, wasps, and birds (such as the hummingbird) that can function as pollinators.

Pollinator Deaths

All pollinators exist as part of a complex ecosystem. Currently, there is not a single problem causing a significant decrease in pollinator populations, but there are dozens of things coming together to cause the larger issue. An ongoing increase of the human population causes more and more natural land space to be taken up by cement jungle. Extreme weather changes and deforestation throughout the world contribute to the declining numbers of pollinating birds and insects, particularly the Monarch butterfly. Without regular intervals of pollinator plants to sup from, butterflies and other pollinators must travel at increasing distances over urban areas that contain a dwindling supply of food sources.

Bees have been particularly hit hard with colony collapse disorder. This condition has been studied extensively, and it has been discovered that large quantities of home and agricultural pesticides and fungicides are clinging to the pollinators and are brought back to hives and nests, causing illness and death. Beekeepers have discovered that beneficial bacteria residing in the guts of honeybees has acquired a resistance to tetracycline, an antibiotic used by

Formula Box

Fantastic Sunny-Spot Pollinator Flowers

- Ageratum
- Alyssum
- Angelonia
- Lantana
- Lavender
- Mint
- Nicotiana
- Oregano, Greek
- Sage
- Salvia
- Spanish daisy
- Verbena
- Zinnia

← Using a combination of creative painting and vertical placement of the hydroponic living wall pollinator gardens makes an original design solution.

the beekeepers to avert colony-destroying infections and devastating bacterial diseases. Additionally, parasitic flies have begun laying eggs within the bodies of live bees, causing millions of deaths. Bees have also been attacked by a virus in recent years caused by another parasitic mite known as the varroa destructor. This bloodsucking parasite transmits deformed wing virus (DWV) directly into the bloodstream of the bee as it feeds. Sadly, this means that DWV bypasses all the bee's natural immunity defenses and swiftly attacks the bee's system. Combined, these devastating issues create colony collapse disorder.

All of these deadly changes to the pollinator's ecosystem, both natural and human-caused, come together to attack the pollinators where they live and destroy their feeding corridors and colonies. These devastating acts could also be the future downfall of the world's primary food sources.

Cooling Heat Islands and Building Corridors

One thing we can do to help the pollinators is build planted corridors through our communities that allow pollinators to sip from organic, chemical-free garden areas as they cross over and through large metropolitan areas. These corridors will help support a healthier pollinator population.

Cities and urban areas are filled with no-fly zones for pollinators and are known as "heat islands" because of the low percentage of trees and vegetation and high percentages of cement walls, parking lots, and buildings. Planting trees as well as growing vegetation and pollinator gardens can help cool this environment, as shaded surfaces can be up to 20 to 45 degrees Fahrenheit cooler. This can give pollinators a corridor to travel through city and suburban areas and increase their likelihood of survival. Building living pollinator walls in urban areas will decrease the heat-island effect and also give pollinators a chemical-free place to sup, rest, and survive. Working together to save more pollinators should be an important goal for communities around the world as our own survival is also at stake.

Butterflies are particularly attracted to flowers that are bright and happy. They love shades of orange, yellow, pink, purple, and white, and prefer to feed in sunny, warm areas. Both butterflies and bees need a water source. A small saucer or shallow container of water with a rock or marbles placed in it will be a great location for bees and butterflies to land and drink. Sit a watering saucer near the pollinator living wall to help attract more pollinators.

Apartment and condominium walls make the perfect location in urban areas for organic living wall pollinator gardens as do fences, gates, and doors. If space is tight, it is possible to plant several very small living wall pollinator gardens in succession for an entrance to a garden or as the perfect balcony display.

A HYDROPONIC POLLINATOR GARDEN

I used a commercially sold hanging hydroponic planting system to plant the pollinator garden you see here. Because the flowers that are most attractive to pollinators are fairly thirsty, a hydroponic system makes sense. If you can't find (or don't want to buy) a hydroponic system, you can use any other system you choose as long as you are attentive to the plant maintenance. Remember, this garden isn't about the kind of system you plant it in: it's really about the pollinators.

❶ Measure a level area for the hydroponic garden.

❷ Fasten the wall mounts included with the hydroponic garden kit to the wall.

❸ Plant the 2-inch plugs into the holes in the growing medium. Some plugs might be too short and will need potting soil packed into the hole to bring the plant flush with the face of the growing medium.

❹ Take the cartridge to the sink and run it under water for at least one minute until it is fully saturated.

❺ Leave the cartridge in the sink for 15 minutes to remove excess moisture. Gently shake.

❻ Place the cartridge into the frame by sliding the frame over the tops of the wall mounts to install onto the wall.

❼ Water flowers and herbs every five to seven days by extracting the cartridge and repeating the watering process.

❽ For outdoor installations, organic liquid fertilizer should be applied at a lower rate in the early spring and fall, as plants are coming out or going into dormancy. During these times, fertilizer should be applied at a reduced rate of 2 teaspoons per 1 gallon of water (0.33 ounces per 128 ounces) with every refill. During the active growing season, when plants are developing new leaves and blooming, fertilizer should be increased to 3 teaspoons per gallon of water (0.55 ounces per 128 ounces).

(continued next page)

Spanish daisy, alyssum, and zinnia are used in a planting combination for the hydroponic unit. It is easy to grow plants from seed, but you can use smaller rooted plants as well.

↑ The hydroponic garden kit I used is pretty simple, consisting of two primary parts: the frame and the hydroponic insert.

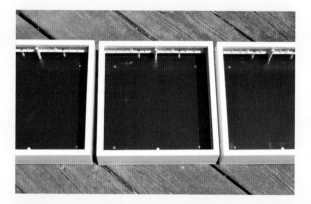

↑ Because the units are smaller than 1 square foot, it is necessary to consider their positioning on the wall in relationship to one another. Purchase one or a dozen and hang them according to your preferences.

↑ Hang the frames with nails. Measure and level the nails first in order to place the units evenly on the wall.

↑ Hang frames in the desired configuration without the hydroponic inserts.

↑ Soak the hydroponic insert in the sink or a tub until it absorbs water throughout the unit. Let it drain before planting.

↑ Cut excess root and soil away from the plant ball, gently pressing the root system tightly together and placing it into one of the holes within the hydroponic system.

↑ Carefully insert the hydroponic unit into the wall frame after the water has drained and excess soil has been cleaned off.

↑ Water the flowers and herbs every five to seven days by pulling the units down, extracting the cartridge, and repeating the root or frame-soaking watering process.

SHADE PALLET GARDEN

Bringing New Life to a Living Wall Using Some Old Wood

PALLET GARDENS HAVE BECOME a popular way to show a young family how urban plant and flower growing can work. These gardens can fit comfortably in most any space; it can give city life a little bit of outdoor planting or country life a little bit of creative-chic style. Reuse a pallet to build a garden and keep it out of a landfill. Whether you have limited room or lots of space, pallet growing can be a surprisingly sustainable experience.

There are many benefits to pallet gardening. It is easy to do, uses very little space, saves money, and reuses a common item. It is estimated that over 200 million pallets are currently in American landfills, and most of the pallets have only been used once. Pallets typically weigh between 35 to 75 pounds, so even shipping the pallets to the landfill is an environmental concern; heavier loads force garbage trucks to burn energy more quickly, and pallets have more weight per square foot than other types of garbage.

When I lived in a tiny apartment in Chicago with a miniscule balcony that barely had enough space for a table, regulations restricted me from hanging plants off the balcony railing. But I could have placed a pallet garden up against the wall in that tight space to bring some growing love into my life. With limited room or lots of space, pallet growing can be a surprisingly sustainable experience, and it is easy to do with a recycled pallet.

Finding Pallets

When selecting a pallet, it is always paramount to know how it was manufactured and where the wood originated if possible. New pallets are often made from scratch at manufacturing factories, large retail stores, and printing facilities. When you go to collect a pallet, ask for the details of what wood was used to manufacture it so you can make an educated decision about bringing it to your apartment balcony or home. If you do not know where a pallet has been, then it could have been exposed to a hazardous material during shipment and might not be the best choice for your home.

In the United States, there are regulations that require pallet manufacturing companies to build pallets treated with chemicals or heat before being shipped overseas. Aside from chemicals, dirty pallets can also harbor mold, bacteria, and pests. Good types of pallets to use for planting projects are those that have been marked "HT." These letters mean the wood has been dried in a kiln and has been heat treated instead of being chemically treated. Pallets can be found by going directly to a manufacturing facility, retail store, or factory. Secondhand pallets are easy to find via the Internet: Freecycle.org, Craigslist.com, and other sites.

At the heart of the sustainable reuse effort is a great concern for safety. Pallets are best used for outdoor vertical gardens, and growing vegetables is not recommended for pallet gardening because of the possibility of chemicals. Flowers and other plants that will not be eaten are the best choice for your pallet garden so that the chemicals are not absorbed through the plant and passed on to you.

Formula Box

**Shade-Loving Plants
Perfect for Your Pallet**

- Begonia, 'Gryphon'
- Coleus, 'Kong'
- New Guinea Impatiens
- Spider plant
- Sweet potato vine, 'Blackie'

Tools Needed

- 2 clean pallets
- Landscape fabric or burlap
- Heavy-duty staple gun
- Staples
- Gloves
- Bricks or landscaping stone
- A level
- Screws and drill/driver
- Zip ties
- Potting soil
- Plants
- Trowel

← This shade-lover pallet garden features plants that adore shade, such as 'Kong' coleus, 'Gryphon' begonia, 'Blackie' sweet potato vine, impatiens, and spider plant.

HOW TO BUILD

A SHADE PALLET GARDEN

1 In this project, we are planting two pallets side by side to give the fairy garden in the foreground a rich, green backdrop. While it is possible to connect the two pallets, it will not enhance their stability. Therefore, treat each pallet as a separate component to the garden. Should you want to sand or paint the pallets with environmentally friendly paint, do so before you start this build. Lay the two pallets on the ground, wearing gloves to prevent splinters. Roll landscape fabric over the backside of the pallet.

2 Staple black landscape fabric or burlap firmly over the backside of the pallet so soil will not escape. Drive heavy-duty staples evenly across the pallet, approximately every 3 inches, to support the soil and plants. Wrap the fabric around the sides of the pallet and staple it down securely. Trim off any excess so the fabric doesn't stick out in front.

3 Using the fabric and staples, build pockets that are around 4 to 6 inches deep to hold soil and plants. Judge creatively where the plants should go on the pallets—it is different for every pallet as each pallet is shaped slightly different, but your focus should be to keep the pockets evenly spaced. Do not worry if the black fabric hangs below the pallet wood; it is supposed to in order to have an appropriate amount of soil with which to plant your garden. Once your plants begin to fill in, the black fabric will not be as noticeable. Try to stretch and staple the fabric in a way that will prevent soil from leaking out the

sides and front. When the inside of the pallet is unreachable with the staple gun, simply staple the black fabric on the edges of the pallet wood. Even stapling means there will be no soil leakage.

4 Use old bricks or landscaping blocks to build a flat, even foundation for the pallets. Recycled landscaping timbers or old concrete sidewalk pieces will also work. Use a level to check the placement of the pallet.

5 Place the pallets on top of your bricks or blocks. Secure the midsection of the pallets to the fence behind it by using zip ties or by screwing them into the wall or fence. Zip ties should be wrapped around the main frame to be secured firmly. To hang the pallet on the wall, predrill holes and screw the pallet directly into the wall or fence. This project will be too heavy to hang off masonry or lightweight wall board, so this technique is recommended for heavy-duty fencing or wooden walls.

6 Purchase plants for your pallet garden. This garden is located in the shade, so I used shade plants that would perform well in lower light conditions. Fill the pallet pockets with potting soil using your trowel. Begin placing plants into the pockets you have created. Plants should be placed snugly for a fuller look as they begin to grow and fill out.

7 Water well and fertilize with organic fertilizer when needed. Maintenance for the pallet garden is simply regular watering and organic fertilizer throughout the season with a clean-out and replant in the spring.

↑ With your pallets on a flat surface, roll landscape fabric over the back face that will be positioned against the wall.

↑ Staple the landscape fabric to the pallet, spacing staples about 3 inches apart, wrapping around the sides and stapling securely. Create pockets on the front of the pallet by stapling landscape fabric in the voids behind the front pallet boards. The pockets should hang down a few inches to create room for soil.

This shade kitchen garden features the florific pallet garden as a colorful backdrop. Featuring some of the plants already in the garden is a good way to make your living wall fit in.

↑ Create a level base for the pallets using extra landscape blocks or other materials that can withstand ground contact. Secure the pallets to the fence or wall.

↑ Fill the pockets with potting soil. Plant the pallets, grouping plants tightly so they fill in visually as soon as possible.

INSULATE-A-WALL GARDEN

Use Flowers, Vegetables, and Herbs to Save Energy

AN EXTERIOR LIVING WALL can help increase the level of energy efficiency operation and can reduce heating and cooling requirements of a building. Having a large number of plants placed on the exterior of the home functions as an additional insulant and can reduce indoor air temperatures by up to 7 degrees Celsius, which means a nearly 20 percent reduction in the heating and cooling requirements.

Studies have shown that the surface of a planted green wall is 10 degrees Celsius cooler than an exposed wall due to the disbursement and absorption of solar radiation as well as the slowing of air movement and carbon dioxide absorption. Mitigating the urban heat island effect, the difference between urban areas and their rural surroundings known to be a huge contributor to climate change, is another benefit beyond traditional energy savings. Vertical gardens truly save energy and conserve resources, but they can also be a gorgeous and eye-appealing contribution to a balcony, patio, or home.

Using a larger wall area, such as a 4-foot to 6-foot wall or fence for planting, means that you can grow a miniature urban farm with hundreds of plants in less than a 7- to 12-inch-wide floor space area. This is a revolutionary idea that could allow unlimited quantities of pollinator plants, vegetables, and herbs in areas of the world where there is minimum space. Entire community gardens could be planted on a 20-foot wall and produce hundreds of pounds of food. Beyond plant production, the conceptual idea of saving money through energy mitigation means that the gardens pay for themselves.

Bigger living walls are definitely better for a building to truly save energy. These walls can fit easily in a home gardener's living area or on an apartment balcony or fence. They can also be used for much larger commercial reasons. Additionally, in many countries around the world, planted living wall systems also qualify for financial reward credits associated with sustainable municipal zoning ordinances and tax credits.

Noise Reduction, Storm Water Management, and Carbon Sequestering

There are other advantages to a large planted wall beyond energy savings, such as reducing noise. Soil, plants, and air surrounding the planting areas are strong acoustic insulators. Noise reduction in a city area or near a noisy street or highway is a great benefit to the occupants of homes and buildings. This is particularly true when a building is located near an extremely loud airport, train, or traffic area. Metropolitan areas also have challenges with storm water management, and large green walls absorb and filter storm water; depending

Formula Box

A Burgundy, Chartreuse, and Yellow Wall Planting Combination That Includes Colorful Vegetables, Herbs, and Flowers

- Basil, purple
- Beets, 'Bull's Blood'
- Calibrachoa, yellows and purples
- Chocolate mint
- Kale
- Lantana, 'Little Lucky Lemon Queen' (or any yellow variety)
- Limelight licorice plant
- Sweet potato vine, 'Marguerite'
- Swiss chard, 'Bright Lights'
- Verbena in purple shades
- Yellow coreopsis

← Living walls can be amazingly beautiful in an outdoor room and are also useful, particularly when used as an insulating wall cover to help save energy.

Plants used for this living wall system include a combination of annuals and vegetables: asparagus fern, purple basil, 'Bull's Blood' beets, cabaret deep blue calibrachoa, cabaret deep yellow calibrachoa, limelight licorice plant, sweet potato vine, Swiss chard, and empress violet charme verbena.

Tools Needed

- Modular planter and bracket system (see Resources, page 152)
- Wall cleats (comes with unit)
- Tape measure
- Level
- Drill/driver and bits
- Screws appropriate for wall type and/or wall anchors
- Container soil
- Organic fertilizer
- Vegetables, herbs, and edible flowers

on the plantings, a living wall can remove pollutants found in the storm water. Watering the green walls with rainwater can save additional money.

Plants are carbon sponges, absorbing or sequestering greenhouse gases from the environment and storing it in their green tissues. The more carbon dioxide that is taken out of the air surrounding the living wall garden, the more oxygen is returned to your neighborhood. While you are saving energy, you are also spreading oxygen, which is good for the health of the community.

Beautiful Growing Results

Insulating living wall gardens can be amazingly beautiful and function as multi-purpose growing solutions as well. Planting a vertical garden that has a diverse selection of vegetables, herbs, and flowers means you will attract more pollinators. More pollinators mean stronger fruit and vegetable production and healthier plants. Most importantly, the beauty of a larger living wall garden can completely transform a patio, balcony, fence, or wall in a magical way; it can bring people to an area that was once flat and unappealing.

Growing many plants in a small floor space will be more successful if you use a wall system that provides for drainage yet has a moisture-retentive potting soil. Plant from seed or use vegetative pack plants that have already been grown, making sure the plants are able to touch and tap into fresh soil within the container system. To maintain the look of the system, allow the plants to fully mature before harvesting. Only harvest about one-third of the plants at a time, allowing them to fully regrow before harvesting a second and third time within the season. By leaving part of the growth available in this rotating harvesting method, the garden will continue to function as an energy-saving living wall. Once you harvest all the plants at the end of the season, you will have pulled the energy-saving benefits out of the soil.

AN INSULATE-A-WALL GARDEN

The tracks and brackets that support your planter units should be fastened directly to the wall or fence. When installed on a wall, attaching wall cleats to at least one stud is recommended.

1 Measure for placement of the units using a level as a guide and marking locations of screws for wall cleats.

2 Predrill a pilot hole slightly smaller than the screw that will be used in the designated locations.

3 Secure the cleats to the wall with fasteners appropriate for your wall type. Use anchors if necessary (on brick or stucco) and ensure that the lip on the wall cleat is facing in the upward direction.

4 Mix the container soil with organic fertilizer and add soil to each unit.

5 Plant vegetables, herbs, and flowers tightly into the modular living wall containers, being sure that all the plants touch the soil mix.

6 Clip the panels and planters onto the mounted wall cleats.

7 Water well.

↑ Be sure that you have all parts required for your planting system. This system includes one bracket, one container, screws, and one wall plaque for each hanging unit.

↑ Because the units are rather small, it is easier to fill them with soil if they are placed closely together on a table or on the ground.

↑ Using a moisture-retentive soil mix (see page 33), fill the container portions of the unit about three-quarters of the way full with soil.

↑ Measure and carefully level the living wall hanging brackets.

↑ Place the brackets side by side to build a close, insulating wall unit with no extraneous spaces between the panels and containers.

← Begin hanging units in the design order most preferred.

↑ Building a wall with an appealing color combination makes the wall marvelously suited to outdoor rooms.

↑ When finished with the hanging process, the units should mold together as a whole and fit tightly together.

To provide a fantastic place to rest the eye as well as the body, consider extending the colorful design with your outdoor room—add accessory containers and plants that coordinate from a color and design perspective with the living wall.

BOOKSHELF FENCE GARDEN

Upcycle an Old Bookshelf into a Shady Living Wall

WHEN ONE OF THE bookshelves in our home became too wobbly and decrepit to support our giant book collection, I saved it to use for an upcycling project—and I had one in mind. I had an empty wall in a shady area of the garden that needed a bookshelf garden attached to it. Rigging it up was quite easy, and as we all know, horizontal surfaces never stay empty long, whether they are in your house or in your garden. Now full of container plants and a few knick-knacks, the shelf is practically beaming. Maybe furniture enjoys fresh air too.

The Joy of Upcycling

What are you throwing in the landfill? Before we became aware, my family would discard just about any item that we no longer needed or wanted. In more recent years, we have worked hard to do everything we can to upcycle, preserve, or reuse every item before recycling. It saves energy and is truly the right thing to do to help our environment. Upcyling is a variance on recycling that means to reuse discarded objects in a way that recreates the product and transforms it into something of a higher quality or value than the original.

In 2012, Americans alone generated about 251 million tons of garbage. Only 87 million tons of this material were composted and recycled, which is equivalent to a 34.5-percent recycling rate. Garbage, or municipal solid waste, is made up of many items people commonly throw away after being used. These items include packaging, grass clippings, food waste, tires, appliances, sofas, bookshelves, and other furniture. While the statistics are strong—Americans recovered over 65 million tons of municipal solid waste via recycling and 21 million tons through composting—we need to recover more to keep our landfills available for the future.

Garbage is a serious global concern; the estimated global municipal solid waste issue will have gone from 3.5 million tons per day in 2010 to more than 6 million tons per day by 2025. If current increases in waste remain unchanged, we will be creating 11 million tons annually by 2100. Not only is there a huge concern about space to keep all this trash, but there is also a concern of expense. Currently the global cost of dealing with municipal waste is a little over $205 billion per year, but it will increase to $375 billion by 2025.

Many people think the solution is burning the trash, but incinerating furniture and other items can release carcinogenic fumes into the environment and increase climactic changes. Landfills also produce heavy levels of methane and other chemicals that are potent greenhouse gases and can contribute to global warming.

The Solution: Reduce, Reuse, and Recycle

This brings us to the solution: intensive reduction of our waste and principles in our communities that encourage reusing and recycling. Why throw out

Formula Box

Annual Plants That Grow Well in Part-Shade Locations

- Basil
- Begonia
- Coleus
- Kale
- Lettuce
- Lobelia
- Mint
- Nasturtium
- New Guinea Impatiens
- Oregano
- Snapdragon
- Spinach
- Sweet potato vine
- Swiss chard

← Converting a shady garden area into a sustainable garden by reusing old materials such as wine bottles and old furniture is easy to do; a living wall can be an active part of the design as a magnet that draws the eye up.

Plants used for this project include begonias of various types, 'Bull's Blood' beets, and sweet potato vine.

Tools Needed

- An old bookshelf
- Extra wood or 2 × 4s
- Handsaw
- Tape measure
- Level
- Drill/driver and bits
- Screws appropriate for wall type
- Paint or stain
- Small potting containers that will fit on your bookshelf
- Container soil
- Organic fertilizer
- Plants

Other Items That Could Be Upcycled into a Wall Garden

There could be an unlimited number of creative ideas for upcycling old items into a wall garden. While I used a bookshelf, you could just as easily use old chairs or small tables that might hold container gardens. Over-the-door shoe organizers form perfect pockets for planting a vegetable garden. Other materials include old metal shelving, Mason jars, old pots and pans, filing cabinets, old clay roofing shingles, cement bricks, louvered shutters, shelving, stairwell supports, tin cans, liter bottles, baskets, fabric pockets, boots, gutters, dressers or desks, and so much more.

All it takes to get started is an old item that can be filled with soil that will not release any type of carcinogenic byproduct into the environment. So, asbestos-filled wall material is not what you are going for—to reuse something successfully, it needs to be a healthy item that will not release anything environmentally harmful into the plants you will be growing. Drill drainage holes into the items that do not have proper drainage and line other items with a nonpermeable lining if you are concerned about soil leakage or other drainage problems.

Growing a beautiful living wall in a nontraditional DIY container is a great way to help the environment by keeping the products out of the landfill. Building unique, beautiful, and creative walls start with the concept of building a better Earth.

something when you can reuse it again in a fashion that prevents the item from going into a landfill?

My garden has become the center for my recycling and reusing efforts. If I cannot donate it to a friend or resale shop, I try to think of a creative way to use old things in my garden. Artistically painted shovels hang on my fence as contemporary art, and you can find rescued Adirondack chairs, wheelbarrows, and old planting containers that I saved from many a garbage can. While some may call it trash, I definitely call it treasure.

Bookshelves are one of those items that can be reused with vigor. Cut the shelves up and use them as spare wood, or make them into a table. Or, in this example, hang the bookshelf and create a rather remarkable living wall to share with garden visitors.

While I have filled the shelves with part-shade annual plants and random artsy tchotchkes, one could just as easily fill the shelves with vegetables and herbs to help feed a family.

A BOOKSHELF FENCE GARDEN

❶ Measure your wall to determine bookshelf placement.

❷ Measure for support wood installation by measuring and marking the wall just below the spot where the top of the bookshelf will rest.

❸ Cut the wood to length for the cleat.

❹ Screw the wood cleat into the fence or wall, using a level on the wall as a reference.

❺ Predrill a hole slightly smaller than the screw used along the top edge of the bookshelf into the cleat.

❻ Secure the bookshelf onto the cleat using the predrilled holes as guides for placement.

❼ Paint or stain the support wood to blend in with the bookshelf.

❽ Mix container soil with organic fertilizer and fill the soil in each planting container.

❾ Plant one plant into each small container, watering well.

❿ Arrange plants on the bookshelf with other tchotchkes in a decorative display.

↑ Hang an old bookshelf on a fence; upcycling it instead of throwing it away saves it from a landfill.

↑ Find planting containers. Here, old tins with plastic inserts are used as small containers that fit the size of the bookshelf.

↑ Fill the containers with soil and plant the living wall garden.

→ While the living wall is not designed to be moved regularly, nearly everything on or surrounding the bookshelf living wall can be moved and relocated at whim. This creates a versatile atmosphere for gardening and entertaining.

SUCCULENT LIVING WALL

These Fleshy Plants Are More Popular than Ever,
Plus They're Perfect for a Living Wall

SUCCULENTS WERE COMPLETELY UNDERAPPRECIATED and outside of my target range of "plants-I-must-have" until author Debra Lee Baldwin penned Designing with Succulents *in 2007. This was a definitive book with astounding photos that helped gardeners worldwide discover succulents as the answer in their busy lives and turned me into a succulent addict. Since then, the use of succulents as centerpiece garden plants has become an international craze, and succulent displays are sold out as soon as they are set out at garden centers. It's a worthwhile addiction, and because of succulents' low water requirements, they are an absolutely brilliant ingredient in a low-maintenance living wall garden.*

Beautiful Beyond Compare

Succulents have remarkable structure and beauty to go with their intense water-saving qualities. They are technically listed as a plant that is a fleshy, thick, water-storage organ. They might store water in stems, roots, or leaves, usually to retain water in arid climates or soil conditions. Cactus are a subcategory within the succulent family, and while cactus are succulents, not all succulents are cactus. Succulents do not have areoles, where the glochids, spines, branches, and flowers might sprout from, and all cactus have them; succulents do not. Therefore, not all succulents have what most people think of as a traditional cactus form.

Succulents, as natives to all sorts of arid areas around the world, have developed fascinating plant shapes and leaf forms with unique colors and complicated designs in their plant structure. This uniqueness gives them an otherworldly appearance that works remarkably well in a living wall. When you think you have discovered all the succulents that ever were, there is another, more stunning plant for you to find. There are succulents that are pointy, narrow, fat, tall, or short; resemble strings of beads, rosettes, paddle leaves; and come in every color one can imagine.

Beauty is the hallmark of the succulent; it captures the eye of every passerby, so they make a delightful wall design. If planted in a moveable system, succulents can easily be moved indoors during colder weather so the living wall could be enjoyed year-round.

Hardiness and Light Requirements

Succulents survive in many different climates. Several types of sedums, for example, can survive seemingly arctic-like winter conditions in the North. However, most exotic succulents found in modern greenhouses and grown for their very unusual shapes and architecture are known to survive in arid climactic conditions. On average, these tough plants can thrive down to 40 degrees Fahrenheit at night but prefer day temperatures that range between 70 and about 85

Formula Box

Great Plant Choices for a Succulent Living Wall Garden

- Burro's Tail (*Sedum morganianum*)
- Hens-and-Chicks (*Sempervivum tectorum* or *Echeveria elegans*)
- Jade plant (*Crassula ovata*)
- Medicine plant (*Aloe vera*)
- Pink vygie (*Lampranthus blandus*)
- Plush plant (*Echiveria pulvinata*)
- Senecio (*Senecio Spp.*)
- Stonecrop (*Sedum acre*)

← Using a small living wall as an accent is an excellent way to draw the eye to an area you want to feature. Creating the wall with succulents means the unit will be drought tolerant and built for harsh gardening conditions.

→ Plants used in this planting arrangement include ghost plant, various types of jade plant, kiwi, pink vygie, blue senecio, and coppertone stonecrop.

Tip

Succulents are extremely drought tolerant, but they appreciate generous summer watering. Let the soil dry out between waterings. Overwatered plants can be mushy, discolored, rotted, and limp; leaves will often turn white, completely losing their color. Underwatered plants will stop growing, turn brown in spots, and then drop their leaves. Consistent, even waterings with time to dry out in between drinks will ensure a healthy plant.

Tools Needed

- 1 bracket-hung framed art wall (see Resources, page 152)
- Screwdriver or drill/driver
- Exterior screws
- Tape measure
- Level
- Cactus or succulent soil mix
- Organic fertilizer
- Succulents
- Trowel

degrees Fahrenheit and average nightly temperatures no lower than 50 and 55 degrees Fahrenheit. This makes the succulent an excellent candidate for most balconies or patios during the summer

Most succulents prefer bright light, but they can scorch badly when placed in direct sunlight. Scorch is easy to diagnose as the leaves will turn brown or even white as the plant bleaches heavily in the sun. Some succulents that get too little light will get leggy and grow out of shape to try to reach the light. Therefore bright, even light is preferred. Many walls, fences, and gates have bright light conditions without direct light, making them an excellent location for succulents.

Good Drainage Is a Must

Consistent soil drainage is the most important condition for growing a drought-tolerant plant such as a succulent. Plant succulents in a quick-draining soil mix that is specifically made for cactus and succulents. If you cannot find the specific soil for purchase, mix 1 part potting soil, 1 part perlite, and 1 part coarse builder's sand in a bucket and use as a succulent potting soil.

Fertilize during the summer with an organic fertilizer recommended for cactus or succulents, following directions on the organic fertilizer container. Winter is not the time to fertilize—stop all fertilization at the end of the summer season.

Building and maintaining a succulent living wall system is remarkably simple. With the succulent's incredibly architectural plant structure and gorgeous color combinations, a succulent living wall can truly add a powerful design statement in a small space. Some succulents have a shallow root system, making them a creative fit in dish gardens as well as wall gardens. Partnering your succulent living wall on the patio with a succulent dish or two on side and dining tables can create a unifying design and a gorgeous outdoor growing setting.

HOW TO BUILD A SUCCULENT LIVING WALL GARDEN

❶ Measure carefully, then assemble your framed art wall system with exterior screws, following the manufacturer's instructions.

❷ Lay the system flat and fill it with the soil mix, using a trowel.

❸ Measure an appropriate amount of organic fertilizer into the soil; mix well.

❹ Arrange the succulents in the container.

❺ Plant the succulents carefully into the soil, being gentle to prevent stem breakage.

❻ Water well while the system is still lying flat.

❼ While the water is draining, attach the mounting bracket to a secure vertical wall, making sure to keep the brackets level and spaced properly.

❽ Hold the planted unit and frame together by placing one hand on the back side of the planter and the other hand on the underside of the frame. The collector tray piece should be at the bottom. Carefully set the planter onto the bracket.

❾ Slide the irrigator into the top planter grooves for watering, then slide the collector tray onto the bottom ledge of the frame to collect any excess water.

❿ When watering in the future, water through the top irrigator unit.

↑ This system is easy to use and has very few parts—it features a top-watering area and a collection box for any dripping water at the bottom of the unit, which helps protect an outdoor wall from excessive watering.

↑ Measure, level, and hang the support brackets for the unit.

↑ This seating area has been converted to an all-succulent design statement with hints of blue to bring out the contrasting copper color in this living wall system and the plants. Once planted, succulents are tremendously easy to maintain

VERTICAL VEGETABLE FARM

Grow Luscious, Fresh Veggies in Even the Tiniest Spaces

I FIRST STARTED THINKING about vertical vegetable growing years ago when standing on a friend's tiny balcony in an apartment building in downtown Chicago. We were up on the eighteenth floor leaning over the railing and conjecturing upon the age-old question, "Would a tomato drop faster than a watermelon to the ground?" when my friend suddenly frowned and said, "I wish I had a garden. I miss green. I crave the smell of real amazing life. Like plants and food and flowers, but I don't have the time or space." We stood quietly for a moment, and I laughed, "You have 3 perfectly good feet to grow a garden here!" We giggled, but it was true. There were 3 tiny feet of space, a meter of worthy gardening potential. Why not grow in every space you can? It's possible to feed your family by growing an urban farm in less than 2 square feet, and I soon discovered how. Although the structure is a unit that a manufacturer made and I purchased, the idea for this Vertical Vegetable Farm really began that night.

Years passed and I continued to consider the issue of how to plant large quantities of food in small spaces. Urban farming is more than a trend; it can be an utter necessity driven by health and financial concerns. Even as organic food is becoming more easily found in grocery stores around the world, to eat exclusively organic is challenging because of the increasing prices for organics in the marketplace. Enabling people to grow in smaller and smaller spaces means that they will be able to provide for their families' health and welfare in a positive way.

Imagining the potential of small-space growing is what got me thinking about the revolutionary planting technique of growing a living wall; planting more than thirty plants in a floor area that is slightly over a square foot—definitely under 2 square feet—is a powerful possibility. All you need is a fence, gate, wall, balcony, or door and a series of window box–style planters, and you can grow amazing quantities of vegetables, herbs, and pollinators. These gardens, along with therapeutic gardens, could solve millions of people's concerns about finding a way to make every meter of space into a whole new level of happiness.

Beautiful Design with Multiple Uses

Best yet, the gardens can be intensely beautiful and amazing conversation pieces, so urban farm living walls become more than just food—they become art. Seeing living art is therapeutic and provides a healthy mental rest in the sea of urban cement and industrial views. Urban heat mitigation and oxygen production are additional benefits, yet the conceptual idea of farming in tiny spaces makes sense that goes beyond beauty and design.

Advantages include no weeds, which means the only regular maintenance for an urban vegetable patio garden is watering and picking the plants. Vegetables and herbs come in a surprising variety of colors, some flowering, some trailing; this plant variety can inspire lovely and colorful designs.

Formula Box

Vegetables and Herbs That Grow Well in a Small Space

- Arugula
- Basil
- Beets
- Celery
- Collard greens
- Kale
- Lettuces
- Mini peppers
- Mint
- Oregano
- Parsley
- Swiss chard
- Thyme
- Pot tomatoes
- Turnips

← Growing many plants in a small space is more than possible; this unit sits directly outside of the living area in this home, bringing a large quantity of fresh herbs and vegetables immediately to the homeowners.

Growing and Harvesting

Patio vegetable production can have challenges; growing a giant indeterminate tomato in a tiny space is not a reasonable structural fit. However, it is very practical to consider growing leafy greens, pot tomatoes, cruciferous vegetables, trailing or vining plants, and all varieties of herbs. Choosing the appropriate plants for a smaller space and the specific light conditions can generate significant success.

Planting on balconies or between tall buildings means considerably less light than a traditional full-sun vegetable garden. Therefore, light considerations must be made when planting vegetables and herbs in a small space. How much light will the garden get? If you have a full-sun area, then planting varieties that include root vegetables and heavily fruiting plants such as small, potted determinate tomatoes or strawberries will be more successful. If you have a shady area, planting fewer root vegetables and fruiting plants and more green leafy vegetables and herbs might be more successful.

Maintaining a vegetable and herb living wall takes consistent watering and fertilizing several times throughout the season. Italian parsley, cilantro, lettuces, and other leafy plants can bolt—that means to flower early—and grow less flavorful and leggy with fewer leaves. Trimming back browning plants, as well as any plants that might have bolted, will keep your garden looking and smelling amazingly fresh.

Design your installation to your preferences; I like to mix burgundy-leaved plants, such as beets or Swiss chard, among the greener plants to give the display visual appeal. Harvest herbs and vegetables for the first time when the plants have reached maturity. Only harvest one-third of the plant at a given time, then wait for that third to grow back before you harvest again.

Tools Needed

- 1 window box living wall system—purchased or built (see Resources, page 152)
- Screwdriver
- Container soil
- Organic fertilizer
- Herbs and vegetables

↓ Plants included in this living wall are beets, two types of kale, peppers, Swiss chard, and turnips.

HOW TO BUILD

A VERTICAL VEGETABLE FARM GARDEN

1. Set up the window box living wall system stand. The one I'm using here has an attached self-watering pump that I hooked up as well.
2. Build the frame by placing screws in predrilled holes and connecting as instructed.
3. Attach the back board assembly.
4. Screw eye hooks into side of the unit (to be used for drip irrigation).
5. Weave the irrigation tubing through the eye hooks and attach irrigation tubing as instructed.
6. Install angled front shelving planting areas.
7. Line the bottom with fabric liner.
8. Lift the vertical wall system up and place it on the stand that has the self-watering pump attached.
9. Connect the drip irrigation tubing.
10. Fill the entire system with soil mixed with organic fertilizer (follow package directions). Fill it from the very top, being careful not to harm the irrigation tubing.
11. Plant vegetables, herbs, and flowers tightly into the planting areas.
12. Attach the timer to the system and assign designated times for drip irrigation.
13. Water regularly.

↑ Add organic soil from the top of the unit. This is most easily accomplished by cutting the bottom of a soil bag and allowing the soil to fall through the back of the unit, layering in height until it is full.

↑ Once full of soil, the window box unit is ready to plant. Gently dig a hole large enough for each root ball to fit on each level of the unit. Start at the bottom and plant to the top.

↑ Set up the unit and incorporate the watering system hosing before adding soil or plants (if the unit you buy or build has a self-watering function).

Water goes here →

↑ To ensure the plants get watered regularly, fill the water reservoir and attach a timer to the unit.

APHRODISIAC WALL GARDEN

Grow Your Own Garden of Love

INTERESTED IN GROWING A living wall that may have certain aphrodisiac qualities? Aphrodisiac-themed gardens offer a creative idea for a living wall garden that is easy to grow and has some enticing added benefits. Using sexually stimulating plants, you combine the sensations that tend to arouse people, such as scent and color, with energy-dense nutrition provided by the garden. Vitamin- and nutrient-rich plants with an herbal-scented kick will be perfect for your special wall garden.

I've thought about the possibility of growing an aphrodisiac garden several times before. In fact, not too long ago, I was standing at the local grocery store considering the ample options in the fruit juice aisle, when an unassuming elderly woman leaned in and began a rather daring discussion on the benefits of vegetables and sexuality. Her opinion was clear: "Passion fruit juice is supposed to be an aphrodisiac, but I think V8 is probably better for you because it has carrots, celery, beets, parsley, lettuce, watercress, and spinach in it. That's a lotta energy to build the excitement." Her comments got me thinking: could we be growing an exciting sex life?

Obviously, discussions about sex are no longer taboo. Times have changed, and the modern-day view of sexuality is a common conversation focused on health and emotional welfare. Herbs and vegetables, we've learned, can improve our sexual appetites, functioning like aphrodisiacs. Aphrodisiacs are most commonly described as food, drinks, or scents that somehow encourage or enhance sexual desire. Historically, foods that resemble human sexual organs have been revered as aphrodisiacs because they sometimes remind us of the phallic or female form. In actuality, sexual vitality has been linked explicitly to nutrition by medical experts. In other words, eating the proper diet can help you get your romance on. Growing your own fresh, organic herbs and vegetables is certainly a great way to do that.

Nutrition

Raw foods are specifically known to greatly enhance sexual energy. In *7 Keys to Lifelong Sexual Vitality*, authors Brian R. Clement and Anna Maria Clement conduct an experiment where they survey four couples and four individuals to better understand their reactions to raw food. Nearly all interviewees lost significant weight and claimed stronger and more intense "desire, arousal, intensity of orgasm, and sexual stamina and performance" by eating a diet that contained between 50 to 100 percent raw foods. The authors suggest in their book that there are several key nutrients essential to sexual health. Consuming these nutrients by eating raw foods is a fantastic way to kick off the romance in your life. At the top of the list are beta-carotene, calcium, choline, iron, niacin, vitamin E, and zinc. Most of these vitamins and nutrients can be found in green

Formula Box

Plant Suggestions for an Aphrodisiac Garden of Love

- Basil
- Beets, 'Bull's Blood'
- Celery
- Cilantro
- Cucumber
- Fennel
- Kale
- Leafy vegetables
- Mint
- Parsley
- Swiss chard

← An aphrodisiac garden features herbs and vegetables with enticing scents and qualities that stimulate the sexual imagination and appetite.

leafy vegetables, kale, cabbage, broccoli, turnip greens, parsley, and Swiss chard. Imagine plucking these nutritious foods directly from your living wall garden and consuming them immediately as a salad for an energy boost.

Other experts agree with this survey's findings that food filled with good nutrition helps our bodies perform more optimally. For example, according to Dr. Stephen Holt in his 1999 book *The Sexual Revolution*, nutrients can be an important point to sexual vitality: "In my own clinical experience, I have seen individuals reverse sexual problems by balancing their diet and taking well-selected dietary supplements. Certainly they may have changed their lifestyle in other ways to enhance sexual function, but good nutrition is the foundation for continuing good sex."

Scent

Smells can be intensely sexy. Helen Yoest has published an entire book on the subject of aphrodisiac plants called *Plants with Benefits*. She gives great emphasis to health- and vigor-promoting plants in the book and explains scented herbs and sweet-smelling plants that can be eaten or inhaled that offer the body a combination of stimulation and aromatherapy. Helen suggests plants such as basil, cilantro, cucumber, fennel, lavender, mint, rose, sage, and jasmine.

Additionally, in the late 1990s, the Smell and Taste Treatment and Research Foundation in Chicago, Illinois, did a study to discover which scents sexually aroused participants. They did this by measuring the blood vessel reaction in erogenous zones of both men and women while the subjects smelled various scents. The studies demonstrated that for both men and women, licorice and cucumber scents are particularly powerful sexual stimulants. Fennel and basil often have a slight licorice scent, which can explain why fresh tomato and basil dishes make our hearts beat a little faster. Having fresh basil of various sorts in a living wall garden or a single fennel plant set at a perfect angle for touching and smelling as you walk by can be two great aphrodisiac garden candidates.

Color

Gardeners often refer to gorgeous photos of gardens as "plant porn." Perhaps we can redefine that term to include healthy plants that lead to healthy aphrodisiac eating that leads to, well, good sex! Building a beautiful living wall also means that your secret pleasure garden can be eye-catching and visually stimulating. Color can also be important to visual stimulation. Warm colors such as red and shades of burgundy or purple can stimulate a warmer reaction from viewers. Consider mixing leafy plants in the living wall planting boxes that might have red and purple. To create an optimal reaction, hang the garden within visual and touching distance on your patio or balcony so you or passersby can reach out and brush their hands through the seductive scents.

Gardening in its purest sense also encourages exercise, which is a stimulating activity for all involved. To encourage the sexy theme with the garden, why not hang and plant the garden with your spouse or partner? Discussing the purpose of the plants in the garden while playfully planting the living wall with your partner is sure to bring a lot of emotional meaning to your shared goal of the garden helping build excitement in your relationship.

Aphrodisiac plants included in this planting are chocolate mint, cucumber, fennel, and variegated mint.

AN APHRODISIAC WALL GARDEN

The hanging brackets for your system should be mounted directly to your wall or fence. When attaching to a wall, wall cleats should be attached to at least one stud.

❶ Measure for placement on the wall or fence, using a level for reference. Mark locations of screws for the wall cleats with a pencil in the small holes of the cleats.

❷ Predrill a hole slightly smaller than the screw used in the designated locations.

❸ Secure the cleats to the wall with screws that are appropriate for your wall type. Use anchors if necessary (on brick or stucco walls) and make sure the lip on the wall cleat is facing upward.

❹ Mix container soil with organic fertilizer and fill each unit with soil.

❺ Plant vegetables and herbs tightly into the Compoclay containers, being sure that the plants touch the soil mix. Press the roots tightly together. Place the tallest plants toward the inside of the container and cascade the plants toward the outside and front.

❻ Clip the panels and planters onto the mounted wall cleats.

❼ Water well.

↑ Planting an aphrodisiac garden starts with good organic soil and an appropriate hanging system, such as Compoclay units.

↑ Add organic planting mix to each container.

↑ Before hanging, set the preplanted units up to inspect and evaluate the design. There should be no plants hanging off the back or blocking the hanging frame.

↑ Before attaching the hanging bracket, be sure it is level.

↑ Predrill holes for unit placement.

↑ Attach the hanging bracket to the wall using screws.

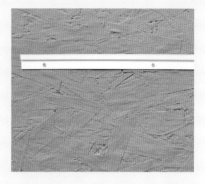

↑ Attach all the frames to the wall, carefully spacing and measuring for accuracy.

↑ Hang one container unit, then hang a panel based on your preferred design pattern.

→ Water plants well after hanging, then water regularly to maintain the living wall.

FREESTANDING ENTRANCE GARDEN

A pretty Project to Improve Curb Appeal with Houseplants

DURING THE WINTER WE stay huddled inside next to our houseplants as if they are little lifelines and hold on to every green bit of life we can. In the spring we explode outside with a passion and vigor seen only by the desperate, hoping to breathe some long-awaited fresh air. As we go out, so do the houseplants. They suddenly appear on patios and balconies as soon as the last frost is done, excited to live it up by soaking in a bit of the natural air and light. Using container or living wall gardens as a way to improve curb appeal and to help oxygenate the areas around the front door can result in an appealing dual purpose for our winter houseplants.

Curb Appeal

Curb appeal is the conceptual idea of improving the look of the front of your home. Realtors and investors use this term as it often goes hand in hand with improving the financial value of the home as well. There are many ways to increase property curb appeal, such as painting the door and shutters, upgrading the mailbox, replacing the siding, installing new house numbers, or upgrading light fixtures. One of the most significant things you can do to increase the value of your home is to add appealing plants. This can be done via landscaping or container and living wall additions and can play a surprisingly important role in property valuation.

Container planting, living walls, and landscaping have an exceptionally positive recovery value if you have put your home on the market—your overall home value can be increased by anywhere from 7 to 15 percent just by having attractive plantings. This means that a nice-looking wall garden can be added with confidence to the list of curb appeal components for your home.

To improve curb appeal, the living wall garden needs to be seen from the street. An excellent location is near or next to the entrance of your home. This area is commonly shaded or has an overhang that might provide bright light without scorching direct sun. If that is the case for you, the perfect plantings could be houseplants, herbs, or vegetables. Houseplants provide a surprising and unexpected planting combination. Recycling old houseplants into a solid living wall will help create a lively view at the entrance to the building.

Fresh Air

Beyond curb appeal, this is also a magnificent idea for decorating outside sliding doors or windows as the plants help filter the air surrounding these living areas. Plants breathe in carbon dioxide and breathe out oxygen, so every time you walk in and out of the house, you get a beautiful, green, stress-free view with an added breath of fresh air.

While plants with larger leaves are more likely to produce high levels of oxygen, all plants create oxygen as a byproduct of the photosynthesis process. This "breathing" is why forests are so important in maintaining Earth's atmosphere.

Formula Box

NASA's Recommended Chemical-Absorbing Houseplants

- Aloe
- Chinese evergreen
- Chrysanthemum
- Dracaena
- English ivy
- Gerbera daisy
- Golden pothos
- Peace lily
- Philodendron
- Snake plant
- Spider plant

← Entrance gardens have always been a way to improve curb appeal and increase fresh air around the door area of a home. Having a living wall entrance garden is appealing and uniquely beautiful.

→ Plants used in this planting unit are mostly tropical and houseplants. Selections include albo fern, begonia, fittonia, heart leaf fern, golden moss, lemon button, peacock moss, peperomia, purple passion plant, rabbits foot fern, spider plant, and toothed brake plant.

Tools Needed

- 1 felt wrap living wall kit or comparable (see Resources, page 152)
- Extra soil
- Hammer
- Nails or L-hooks
- Black window screening
- Scissors

The Associated Landscape Contractors of America (ALCA) and the National Aeronautics and Space Administration (NASA) conducted a two-year study to determine ways to create breathable atmosphere in outer space. Their research demonstrated that tropical plants are very effective at processing carbon dioxide as well as other gases and chemicals. Their list of recommended plants for reducing toxic chemicals in indoor environments might not have as strong of an effect in an outdoor environment where the circulation of the air is constantly replaced. However, any absorption is better than none and walking by a beautiful living wall that is specifically built to remove harmful chemicals and return fresh oxygen is a great thing for your family.

Growing Houseplants Outdoors

Most houseplants are fairly low maintenance and offer little trouble. Many gardeners prefer bringing the plants outside during the spring and summer to give them some fresh air and different humidity. Watering houseplants with rainwater seems to perk them up after their long winter season as well.

Once planted in their new location, they require only that you give them the proper light, keep an eye out for pests, water regularly while letting the soil dry out between waterings, and regularly fertilize with a light organic fertilizer. Succulents and arid desert plants require far less water than other typical houseplants. Using a self-watering system can keep the living wall system low maintenance for an active family.

Planting houseplants in a living wall by using the Florafelt Vertical Garden System is easy. The technique is different than typical plantings as you will be wrapping the roots of each plant to create individual pouches of tightly wrapped soil and root that are placed inside the Florafelt planter pockets. When warm weather is over, it is easy to relocate this freestanding garden inside next to a sunny window for continued enjoyment through the winter season.

HOW TO BUILD

A FREESTANDING ENTRANCE GARDEN

Vegetables need a consistent supply of water, so I chose to use a vertical wall kit with a recirculating water pump that delivers a steady and controllable supply of water to the top of the unit (see Resources, page 152). I'll show you how to hook up this kind of system on the next couple of pages. I think these self-watering systems are the best choice for veggies, but naturally you can plant the veggie garden you see here in any system of hanging planters or freestanding boxes you choose. Just remember to water regularly—the soil in containers dries out much faster than the ground.

1. Measure the wall to make sure the system you're using will fit where you want to locate it.
2. Using L-hooks or nails, hang the vertical wall kit so the bottom of the wall garden hangs into the black water tank by 1 inch.
3. Firmly stretch open the pockets.
4. Use root wrappers provided with system to wrap the plants so they can be changed out if needed.
5. Start with a diamond shape.
6. Fold the top corner down to create your top soil line.
7. Place your plant facing forward. Add a couple table-spoons extra soil if needed.
8. Fold the bottom corner up.
9. Fold the bottom edge up over the roots.
10. Push the planting unit down, squishing slightly. Hold down the edges and fold in the tips.
11. Use a rubber band to hold it together (optional).
12. Place plants into stretched pockets, pushing down firmly so the wrapped plant is entirely enclosed within the pocket.
13. Plug in the timer. Suggested watering time is 30 minutes per day.
14. Maintain the water level below flap.
15. Add screening to keep mosquitoes out of the water tank.

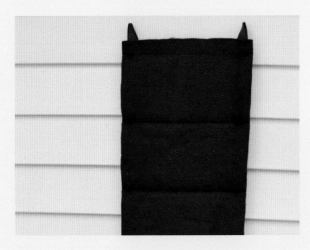

↑ Unpack the planting unit from its shipping box and find a site that works well for you. Hang the unit using two nails.

↑ Lay a felt root wrapper on the ground at a diagonal and place the plant in the top portion of the square.

↑ Fold up the bottom corner of the square.

↑ Pull the square up and place the folded bottom along the top of the plant. Press down on the rootball to flatten it.

↑ Fold one side of the root wrapper over, then the other.

↑ Although it's not necessary to wrap it with a rubber band to hold it together, it's still a good idea to reinforce the wrapper by binding it until it is stuffed into the unit.

↑ Stuff each wrapper into a pocket in the unit starting at the bottom, working up the wall garden.

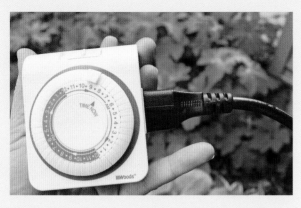

↑ Plug in the timing unit so the automatic watering system waters the living wall once per day for 30 minutes per day to start. It can be adjusted if more or less water is needed.

↑ Plug the water pump's power cord into the timer.

↑ Fill the water reservoir, then nestle the pump down into the water at the bottom of the reservoir, adjusting the wiring to rest behind the felt.

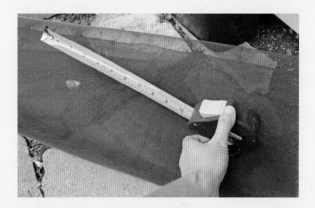

↑ If mosquitoes are a problem in your area, install a mosquito screen. Simply measure a black screen and cut to the same width as the reservoir.

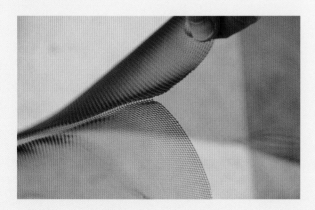

↑ Fold the screen so it does not pop out of the reservoir but stays just above the surface of the water when the reservoir is filled.

↑ In addition to keeping mosquitoes out of the reservoir, the screen collects droppings from the plants, so rinse it every time you add water.

CULINARY KITCHEN GARDEN

Grow Your Own Organic Vegetables and Herbs for Cooking

WHILE INTERVIEWING A YOUNG mother in an urban inner-city area, I listened as she told me a heartbreaking story. Her son had asthma, and medications were not effective, so she tried limiting his chemical exposure by providing more organic food. The price of organic vegetables from the market was high, and she dreamed of having a garden where she could grow her own fresh produce. There were two places she could grow: her small balcony or a fence along a back alley that was over 20 feet long but offered only a 3-foot-wide area to walk.

Finding a practical and easy growing solution for people who have small, narrow spaces, like this young mother, seemed impossible until recent years when living wall systems have become readily available. At 18 inches by 8 inches, the modular vertical planters in this project take up exactly 1 square foot of space. Thirteen units could be placed side by side on the 20-foot alley wall the woman had to work with. She could easily stack five or six planters on top of each other, expanding her planting space to 65 square feet if she planted thirteen units wide, five units tall. Sixty-five square feet of food for her family, a larger garden than many traditional land gardens in backyard garden spaces. Even by utilizing only a small area of the wall and planting traditional containers beside the wall garden, a massive quantity of vegetables could be grown in a narrow area.

The herbs and vegetables that are most popular are ones easily and quickly grown. Great examples include leaf vegetables such as Swiss chard, lettuces, kale, arugula, celery, and almost any variety of herb. Basil, chives, cilantro, and oregano are all fast-growing herbs that contribute heavily to culinary in nearly every culture.

Food grown on living walls can be a solution for urban areas worldwide and a revolutionary concept for community gardens and apartment buildings. Imagine coming together as a community to grow healthier food and the positive change that can happen within a community as a result of the effort.

Finding a Location

While there is no garden or growing system that is completely perfect, there are many that offer creative solutions for growing in small spaces. While urban and city dwellers need these solutions, so do suburbanites and farmers. I grew up in Indiana farm country, and when I recently went back to a garden center to speak on growing, the number one question asked by farmers was, "How do I grow without chemicals?"

When I asked them what they meant by that since they have large plots of land to grow on, I discovered that farmer families or their neighbors typically have a large garden out in a back area of the property. This area is near the

---

Formula Box

Common Culinary Plants for Kitchen Gardening

- Basil
- Celery
- Chives
- Cilantro
- Kale
- Lettuce
- Mint
- Oregano
- Parsley
- Spinach
- Swiss chard
- Thyme

← Attractive as well as functional, a culinary kitchen garden can be incorporated into a small space yet provide an enormous amount of fresh vegetables for a family and community.

Plants used in this kitchen culinary design include basil, beets, celery, mint, purple basil, and Swiss chard.

fields—only a few feet away from them, in fact. These corn and soybean fields are not organic and are sprayed with massive amounts of fertilizers, insecticides, and herbicides. This overspray drifts to nearby gardens, giving the neighbors a heavy dose of chemicals in their growing area.

When the farm properties were tested, areas toward the center of the property were less likely to be exposed to chemical overspray. On average, most homeowners or farmers who own a large amount of land primarily keep their homes and buildings in the center of their property. So if a garden was installed closer to the buildings, farmers would have more success growing with less chemical exposure.

Finding a small growing space on a large property might seem silly, but to families exposed to large quantities of chemicals, it might just be a positive healthy choice that could change their lives. A food garden can yield an estimated ½ pound of fresh produce per square foot of garden area. When comparing freshly grown food with in-season grocery prices, that produce is worth approximately $2.00 per pound or more. Since a traditional garden takes up a larger area and forces growers to use existing soil that could have chemicals trapped in it, building a living wall with fresh, organic soil makes sense. Barn sides, fences, home walls, pens, and gates create fantastic and productive garden areas with lower chemical exposure.

A CULINARY KITCHEN GARDEN

I really like the planting system I'm using here because not only is it modular so you can hang the planters anyway you like, but you can also get a reservoir and self-watering tubes so you know your veggies are getting the water they need. Plus, I think the planters are pretty when they're hung in a group (although the plants will cover them up quickly). For your culinary garden, any planters that can be attached directly to a wall or fence will do. Just think carefully about the arrangement and leave plenty of space between rows for the plants to grow.

❶ Open the living wall package, making sure you have the self-watering tank, planters, and screws.

❷ Save package wrapping for the horizontal self-directing holes template on the package. Using a level and the template, calculate how many wall planters you will need by dividing the width of your wall area by 18 inches and height by 13 inches. For example, four planters cover a 36-inch width and 26-inch height wall area.

❸ Predrill holes.

❹ Attach the self-watering tank to the wall using included hardware. Place the lid on the tank.

❺ Fill planter with living wall potting soil up to the soil level line.

❻ Mix organic fertilizer in with the container soil.

❼ Plant your favorite vegetables and herbs.

❽ When hand-watering, water will seep evenly through breathable vents across the front of planter; carefully dry the planter prior to hanging.

❾ Slide the planter loops up behind and onto tank hooks. Hint: Look down the irrigation supply channel to see the loops and hooks.

❿ Use watering holes for watering unless you are attaching self-watering system.

⓫ If using the self-watering system, pour one liter of water through watering hole into the tank, which will precisely water the plant roots. Fill the reservoir to keep the plants watered for up to two weeks. Breathable vents aerate the soil and release excess moisture from heavy rainfall or excessive watering.

↑ Most vertical hanging planters are super easy to install. This unit includes the containers, watering tank, and screws.

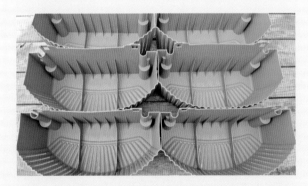

↑ Place all the units side by side when filling for easier soil management.

↑ Fill to the soil level line.

→ Measure and level each unit to make sure the garden will be visually appealing.

→ Plant vegetables, loosening pot-bound roots carefully so that they will spread down into the soil.

↓ Hang each unit below its appropriate water reservoir, being careful not to bend freshly planted vegetables in the process.

↑ Tend to the garden as necessary, removing brown leaves or stems and watering regularly.

← Plants will grow in thickly with time but start out smaller. Harvest one-third to two-thirds of the vegetables at a time, letting the plants grow back for second and third harvests throughout the season.

AROMATHERAPY GARDEN

Invite Some Favorite Scents into Your Garden to Improve Mood

SMELLS TRIGGER MEMORIES AND they can change your mood. For instance, on a gorgeous August morning, mist hangs in the air as I get ready for the first day of school. My house is an island in a sea of cornfields in the middle of Indiana, and I wait on my front porch steps for the bus to come down the angling road and pick me up to drive me 10 miles to school. It is already 80 degrees with 90-percent humidity, and as I sit on the steps, I am enveloped in the scent of Mr. Lincoln—the reddest, most beautiful rose I ever did see and the prize of my father's garden. That rose could lure in any human from 20 feet away with its beautiful, heady, overpowering scent. I would come out early on those first days of school just to have the privilege of sitting next to Mr. Lincoln because his scent was a powerful stimulant. When I smelled this rose, even when my childhood was emotionally complex and filled with drama, I was happy.

Good-smelling things can improve your mood, just as Mr. Lincoln did for me as a child. While aromatherapy is the use of fragrance to enhance health and promote feelings of well-being, there is a limit to the power it has, according to scientific studies. Discussions on essential oil and scents have been going for centuries; Egyptians used odors to treat diseases. Scents are used in modern-day times to relieve pain, reduce chemotherapy side effects, and promote restful sleep. However, the only thing that aromatherapy has been scientifically proven to do is improve mood.

Scientific Proof

A study from the University of Vienna found that female patients displayed less anxiety in dental clinics when orange oil was used. Mie University School of Medicine discovered that smaller doses of antidepressant medications were needed after patients trialed a citrus fragrance treatment. Controlled trials have also suggested that different types of aromatherapy might be helpful for calming symptoms of Alzheimer's disease and dementia. One small study dosed a hospital ward with either water or lavender oil scent for several hours. A researcher unaware of the study's design, who wore a sensory block to prevent inhalation of odors, was sent to rigorously examine the behavior of the residents who all had dementia. Results indicated that lavender oil aromatherapy decreased agitated behavior and encouraged calmness.

Essential oils can have a toxic effect to humans when consumed orally in large quantities rather than inhaled. Various oils can produce illness and even fatal effects, so essential oils should be inhaled or consumed within suggested parameters due to safety concerns. Natural plants, however, do not have that restriction because they have not been distilled down to an essential oil and are safe and beneficial for sniffing. With the knowledge that scents can be mood enhancers—either calming or stimulating—having scented plants in a living wall garden is a powerful way to build a healthier mood.

Formula Box

Scented Plant Ideas for a Living Wall Garden

- Anise hyssop
- Artemesia
- Basil
- Fennel
- Flowering tobacco
- Lavender
- Lemon balm
- Lemon thyme
- Oregano
- Rosemary
- Scented geraniums (every type)
- Thyme

← Whether in an industrial area or in an everyday home, herbs can have a powerful impact on mood. Beauty, as well as scent, can be tremendously uplifting.

↑ Plants included in this aromatherapy living wall include basil, chocolate mint, cilantro, curry, mint, oregano, sage, lemon thyme, and thyme.

Tools Needed

- 1 bracket-hung framed art wall (see Resources, page 152)
- Screwdriver or drill/driver
- Exterior screws
- Tape measure
- Level
- Potting soil
- Organic fertilizer
- Scented plants
- Trowel

Combination Smell Garden Ideas

- Pizza-Scented Culinary Garden: rosemary + oregano + basil
- Calming Garden: lavender + rosemary + mint or mint-scented geranium
- Stimulating Garden: lemon balm + lemon thyme + lemon geranium
- Happy and Relaxing Garden: rose-scented geranium + lavender
- Memory Stimulating Garden: cinnamon geranium + basil + thyme
- Invigorating Garden: mint + anise hyssop + fennel

Improving Mood

In a time when millions worldwide are suffering from stress, mental illness, sleep disorders, and road rage, it seems that improving our mood with scent might be a positive thing. Whether you are at work or home, a scented garden filled with delicious smells located near the patio lunch area, on an entrance door or gate, or perhaps on a wall near a busy entrance makes a lot of sense.

There are several types of plants that can contribute to a scented wall garden. There are flowers that have smells, herbs with strong essences, and foliage herbal plants, such as scented geranium. Depending upon the visual design you prefer, it is possible to use plants in combination with one another to create a certain atmosphere or scent. The Combination Smell Garden Ideas sidebar includes are several different types of scent combinations to consider.

For example, a pizza-scented garden might be positioned on a patio next to the kitchen. You could use the herbs for cooking, and of course, you could stimulate a guest's appetite and create a dining mood with the scented garden.

Growing Scented Plants

Scented geranium is a particularly powerful plant as its smell can fill a room. Like other herbs, scented geraniums are fairly easy to grow. They are delightfully drought tolerant and actually tolerate a wide variety of growing conditions. Their preference is for at least four hours of direct sunlight per day. While other herbs can tolerate far less light, scented geraniums require more light to stay healthy. There are a couple geraniums that are exceptions to that rule: *Pelargonium tomentosum* 'Chocolate Mint' and *Pelargonium tomentosum* 'Peppermint' both tolerate more shade.

While herbs of all kinds would love more sunshine and at least some direct sunlight through the day, most can survive well with bright reflective light and a heavy amount of shade. They may not be aggressive under those conditions, but with a small growing space, it works well. Choose the plants that you like and make you feel good by researching what might work best for your health and home conditions.

Capturing the amazing aromas of fresh herbs either at work or at home can have a profound effect. Creating a small living wall that rests on a door or near an entrance is a great way to welcome people with amazing scents.

HOW TO BUILD AN AROMATHERAPY GARDEN

① Measure carefully, then hang the framed art wall system you're using according to package directions.

② Lay the system flat and fill with the soil mix using the trowel.

③ Measure an appropriate amount of organic fertilizer into the soil; mix well.

④ Arrange your preferred scented plants in the container.

⑤ Water well while the system is still lying flat.

⑥ While the water is draining, attach the mounting bracket to a secure vertical wall, making sure to keep the brackets level and spaced properly.

⑦ Hold the planted unit and frame together by placing one hand on the back side of the planter and the other hand on the underside of the frame. The collector tray piece should be at the bottom. Slowly set the planter onto the bracket.

⑧ Slide the irrigator into the top planter grooves for watering, then slide the collector tray onto the bottom ledge of the frame to collect any excess water.

⑨ When watering in the future, water through the top irrigator unit.

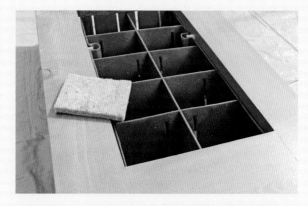

↑ Your hanging framed planter should include spongy planting hole liners to include moisture.

↑ Fill the planting areas with the appropriate soil mix.

↑ Plant the herbs firmly into the soil-filled system.

↑ Flatten larger rootballs.

↑ Backfill the holes with soil as needed to provide a full rooting area for each plant.

↑ Hang the unit by screwing hanging brackets into a wall or, if hanging on a door or gate, use wreath hooks to hang the unit by attaching a wire around the area where the bracket would normally go and hooking the wreath hook onto the wire to hang it in a nonpermanent position. Hanging the living wreaths on doors and gates is a wonderful way to have everyone who comes and goes exposed to the amazing aromatherapy benefits of herbs.

MONEY-SAVING GARDEN

Growing a Fruitful Garden from Seed Is Practically Free

WATCHING MY GRANDMOTHERS GARDEN their plots was perhaps the best way to learn how to be frugal. They reused everything: coffee tins were saved to hold and sort seeds and tools, tomato stakes were old broom sticks, watering cans were old buckets, pie tins were tied to stakes in the garden to keep away pests, compost tea was handmade from old sheep dung, and pantyhose cut up into strips was used to tie up bean plants. There was no waste in those gardens. Dead plantings and rotted vegetables were used to make compost, and no potting soil was ever needed as soil from the old sheep barn was filled with more healthy microbes than any manufactured soil. They planted everything from seed—it was a money-saving garden.

Waste seems to be a modern invention, and waste creates expense. Finding a way to annually reuse items is a green and money-saving idea. Most living wall systems can be stored over winter and brought out to be used repeatedly for many seasons. After the initial purchase of a living wall system, it can truly bring long-term enjoyment if maintained properly. Vegetative plants cost more to purchase. Greenhouses have to maintain and grow them for many weeks by the time you are ready to buy them and plant them in your garden. While it might take more planning, there are two ways to use fresh seed. When saving money is the goal, costs can really be cut for the living wall garden by using seed over vegetative grown plants.

Sow Seeds Directly in the Living Wall Soil

There are several easy-to-grow flowers and vegetables that are simple to sow directly in the soil of the living wall container. Start by working your preferred organic fertilizer or soil amendments into your soil. Add the soil to the living wall system, then gently water. This helps the seeds to stick to the soil where you place them. Plant the seeds according to the directions on the seed package—some seeds require light to germinate and must be placed at the top of the soil, and some seeds require a deeper planting. If you have enough space and want a straight planting row, use a garden row marker tool to make it straight. The tool allows you to stretch out string between two garden dibbers to dig a small furrow that helps guide seed planting along the straight line. Whether you choose planting rows or more clustered planting in a living wall pocket is really based on what your final design goal might be.

Generally speaking, seed placement can be important for a living wall; plants that hang over and grow lush should be planted at the front edge of the planting pocket so the plant can spill over the edge. Fuller, medium-sized plants do well in the middle of the planting pocket and function as a filler for the center of the planting area. Tall plants should be placed at the back of the pocket so that their height can peek out from behind the other plants and also cover some of the blank wall behind the system.

Formula Box

Easy Plants to Sow Directly in Soil from Seed

- Allysum
- Beans
- Beets
- Carrots
- Cucumber
- Kale
- Leaf lettuce
- Love-in-a-mist
- Mini sunflower
- Nasturtium
- Radishes
- Spinach
- Sweet peas
- Swiss chard
- Zinnia

← Living walls can also be money-saving gardens if seeds are incorporated into the growing plan. This living wall is filled with color that offers a happy mood lift to passersby, and at least half of the plants are grown from seed, which saves significant money.

OPTION: Start Seeds Inside before Frost

Many flowers and vegetables cannot be grown through cold winter conditions due to their frost sensitivity. Starting plants indoors from seed six to eight weeks before the last frost guarantees that seedlings will have an advanced start to the growing season. Instead of seeing empty soil in your living wall, you will be able to plant a seedling in the living wall after the last frost of the season. Getting a head start on growing means you will have flowers or vegetables produced much sooner than if you had planted seeds directly into the soil.

Seeds and seedlings are quite delicate, so having a lighter soil to start your seeds in often means better success. Using a seed-starting soil mix, plant seeds according to package directions. Plant in a starting kit, in cell packs from last season, or even in old yogurt containers. Make sure that the containers you grow in have good drainage, because if the plants are too wet they will rot. Grow the planted seeds in a warm area between 60 and 70 degrees Fahrenheit, preferably in a sunny window or beneath a fluorescent light. If you use artificial lighting, the seedlings need close exposure—put the light only three to four inches above the seedling tray.

Following the directions on the package, place seeds in or on soil, then water delicately with a spritzer. Cover with cellophane or a clear plastic tray top to help hold in humidity. Mist daily and watch for sprouting. Once the plants sprout, uncover the seeds and begin watering from the bottom—pour water in at the bottom of the tray instead of the top. Heavy top watering when seedlings are young can cause "damping off," which means the seedlings will rot. Watch the weather closely and do not put the seedlings out before the last frost as the plants could die if it is not warm enough outside.

About Seeds and Storage

Fresh seeds have a longer shelf life. Each package should be dated for the current year, if possible, to guarantee success. Seeds are sold in several differing forms: pelletized, loose, and in tape form. Sold in packets, loose seeds are most familiar to gardeners. Pelletized seeds look like small pills, as they are individually coated to make handling and proper spacing much easier. They are also sold in small packets. Seed tapes also work successfully in living wall pockets. They are long strips of biodegradable paper with seeds embedded within the strip. These embedded seeds are properly spaced, so you do not have to worry about spacing when planning; just unroll the tape and cover with soil.

Airtight jars or kits built to file seed packets alphabetically away from air or moisture are perfect places to store extra seeds. When stored properly and placed in a clean, dry location, seeds can remain viable for several years.

Planning your living wall garden with seed means you can create a more affordable garden. I used seeds to build a pollinator garden to attract bees and butterflies, which include alyssum and zinnia seeds mixed with vegetative sweet potato vine. Saving money can look gorgeous.

Plants used in this living wall unit include 'Chipotle' sweet potato vine, 'Marguerite' sweet potato vine, white sparkle euphorbia, clear crystal white alyssum, white wedding zinnia, cosmic red cosmos, and cosmic orange cosmos.

A MONEY-SAVING GARDEN

❶ Choose a spot with the right amount of sunlight for the seeds and plants you have chosen.

❷ Use a level to draw a reference line and make sure the wall garden will be straight. However, if you're installing on a fence and your fence line slopes slightly, your garden may look better if you install it parallel to the top of the fence.

❸ Mark where the grommet holes in the planting pouch will be for the top row, then follow with each consecutive row.

❹ When hanging multiple pockets, overlap the pockets' grommets horizontally. Space them the correct distance apart vertically from grommet to grommet—this hides the grommets and ensures plants have enough space to thrive but are still dense enough to create a lush living wall!

❺ Predrill the holes.

❻ Slide fasteners into the holes.

❼ Attach the pockets with the fasteners.

❽ Fill pockets halfway with potting soil using your trowel. If installing automatic drip irrigation, install behind the pocket tongue. Test the entire system prior to adding soil. Once soil has been added, adjust the drip lines so that they are above or at the soil line, then adjust if additional soil is needed.

❾ Plant the seeds according to the directions on the seed packs, keeping plants that hang over and grow lush at the front edge of the pocket, plants that grow full at the middle of the pocket, and plant seeds that grow taller at the back of the pocket.

❿ Water through the tongue with 2 cups of water per pocket, being careful not to disturb the seeds. Once the plants start to grow, water gently with a water wand or use an automatic drip irrigation system. Remember to only water the top tongue; don't water the plants directly.

↑ Hang the planting pockets with screws driven into the wall or fence.

↑ Using a level, make sure the units rest side by sid. Half fill with soil, and backfill as needed once the plants are installed.

↑ While it is possible to use only seed, I chose to mix vegetative plantings and seeds. Fill with any vegetative plantings first, leaving areas for the other seeded plants to fill in.

↑ Plant seeds, such as these zinnia seeds, according to directions.

↑ Regular organic fertilization throughout the season will encourage plant growth, particularly for heavy-feeding plants such as annuals.

The garden's bright orange, creamy white, and bold purple design is meant to stimulate a colorful setting for an outdoor room.

SMART GARDEN

A Balcony Garden Can Help Increase Your Attention Span in Your Home Office

YEARS AGO I LEFT a dramatic and hated job to begin a new life working out of my home office. While it might seem terrifying to some, it was a miracle for me—it allowed me to step away from the pain and drama of a closed-in, unhealthy environment and transform my office into something healthier. While I spend a lot of time writing in front of my computer inside, I have built a lovely view of the trees and sky. When I am able, I work outside on my balcony or patio—I try to surround myself with plants and life. It does more than make me happy; it helps me breathe and think. Having a close connection to plants while you are working, particularly in a home office, can mean the difference between a positive working environment and a horrid one. That's why I planted this smart garden, and one like it can do the same for you.

Plants Sharpen Your Brain

Scientific American recently ran an article discussing the power of plants on the brain based on a study done by the *Journal of Environmental Psychology*. Researchers demonstrated that when a working office setting has plants, it boosts the office workers ability to maintain attention. Additionally, there was a study done at The Royal College of Agriculture in Circencester, England, showing that students demonstrated 70 percent greater attentiveness when their classrooms contained plants. These results are based on a specific concept: attention restoration theory. Rachel and Stephen Kaplan developed the conceptual idea for the theory, and according to attention restoration theory, people can pay attention and have a greater capacity to pay attention to work if that person has had longer exposure to plants or nature. In other words, you can pay attention more when you have an emotional or physical connection with nature.

Combine this scientific information with what we already know about plants and oxygen; that, as part of their breathing process, plants output oxygen in exchange for carbon dioxide. Having plants in a living wall sharpens our attention, produces fresh oxygen, and also offsets chemicals and purifies air, as demonstrated by the study done by the Associated Landscape Contractors of America (ALCA) and the National Aeronautics and Space Administration (NASA). Plants can make a positive difference for our work environments.

Working at Home

The number of telecommuters or at-home workers is increasing worldwide. According to a poll conducted by Reuters, nearly "one in five workers around the globe, particularly employees in the Middle East, Latin America, and Asia, telecommute frequently and nearly 10 percent work from home every day." While working conditions within an office can be high-pressure or uncomfortable, when workers are able to telecommute, they can take control of their working environment in a unique way.

Formula Box

Top Houseplants for a Living Wall Garden with Dim or Low-Light Exposure

- Arrowhead vine
- Cast iron plant
- Chinese evergreen
- Dracaneas
- Peace lily
- Peperomia
- Philodendron
- Pothos
- Snake plant
- Spider plant
- Zee Zee plant

← Simply being exposed to a garden during work hours can improve one's outlook; building a small living wall filled with oxygenating plants can contribute to that positive experience by bringing nature to a balcony or patio.

↑ This planting design uses a mix of tropical plants selected for their color and attractiveness. They include arrowhead, croton, hypoestes, ivy, schefflera, and spider plant.

Tools Needed

- 1 bracket-hung framed art wall (see Resources, page 152)
- Screwdriver or drill/driver
- Exterior screws
- Measuring tool
- Level
- Potting soil
- Organic fertilizer
- Scented plants
- Trowel

At-home workers have more freedom to manage family and home because they are able to work the personal hours that make them feel better and in control. Are you a night owl? No problem; working at home enables you to pull more night hours. Are you an early bird? No problem; get up at 4:00 a.m. and jump online to send a few emails. Telecommuting and working at home is also more sustainable because telecommuting reduces carbon dioxide and ground-level ozone levels by at least 25 percent. If 40 percent of the US population would work at home half of the time, it would be like taking 9 million cars permanently off the road.

Make the Balcony, Terrace, or Patio Your Office

Blending the work-at-home freedom with more natural conditions means working in the home can actually be better and healthier for you, your corporation, and the environment. Particularly if you take your work to the terrace or balcony. Winter might restrict balcony office work, but three seasons of the year could easily be spent outside on a balcony. With modern-day laptops, it might not even be necessary to have a traditional table or desk. Put together a chair, plants, and a living wall with a place to rest your coffee cup, and you have built a small outdoor office space that might free your soul and your mind to make amazing work progress.

In the United States alone, Forrester Research has forecasted that 34 million Americans currently work at home, and the number is projected to increase to over 65 million by 2016. Working in the home saves large companies time and money. Best yet, it increases the happiness levels of many of the workers that participate in this type of working arrangement. Having a traditional home office with an escape to a nature mindset leads to amazing ideas for your summer office. Create a living wall with houseplants, vegetables, or herbs—whatever your favorite plants might be—on your balcony or patio. Keep the living wall on the balcony or patio close to your work zone to enable the most benefits from the experience. Using houseplants might give you the added benefit of moving the wall garden inside to your primary office area during the winter as well.

Working outside on a computer, whether on a covered patio, balcony, or in open area, can sometimes mean that there is glare on your computer. This can be mitigated by installing bamboo screens or a canvas canopy over your work area. Building a large or small living wall in a shaded area that is for low light, accompanied by a mix of tall potted houseplants, can help block glare, absorb street sound, and still provide healthy plants. Combine a home office with a patio, terrace, or balcony for a happier work experience.

HOW TO BUILD
A SMART GARDEN

1. Measure carefully, then hang the framed art wall system according to package directions.
2. Lay system flat and fill with the soil mix using the trowel.
3. Measure an appropriate amount of organic fertilizer into the soil; mix well.
4. Arrange your preferred plants in the container.
5. Water well while the system is still lying flat.
6. While the water is draining, attach the mounting bracket to a secure vertical wall, making sure to keep the brackets level and spaced properly.

7. Hold planted unit and frame together by placing one hand on the back side of the planter and the other hand on the underside of the frame. The collector tray piece should be at the bottom. Slowly set the planter onto the bracket.
8. Slide the irrigator into the top planter grooves for watering, then slide the collector tray onto the bottom ledge of the frame to collect any excess water.
9. When watering in the future, water through the top irrigator unit.

↑ Design the layout of the plants by placing the framed system side by side with the plants and calculating the best color arrangement for the planting pockets.

↑ Once filled with soil, place the plants in the soil pockets and backfill with extra soil. Water well.

↑ Using brackets, hang the unit firmly on the wall and keep it regularly watered.

↑ Building a living wall that can also function as an air-freshening natural resource for a modern work-at-home family can bring both beauty and health inspiration.

COLORFUL LIVING WALL

Build One Today Because Beauty Is Important

WHEN I FIRST BEGAN gardening, my color palette was heavy with a monochromatic theme of green on green. It seemed to reflect simplicity and calmness. Many shades of green foliage seemed to blend in a rolling wave of chartreuse green to Kelly green to blue-green; it was a wave of color calming to the eye and heart. As my garden has matured, I have expanded the color palette to include flowers of all shades and an explosion of bold foliage colors. Each garden bed, garden container, and garden wall has grown into a design challenge. Part artistic expression and part mystery, I am excited to see what develops with each experiment. How shall I make this garden more filled with passionate color?

Beautiful Gardens Improve Community

Simply having a garden for its beauty is as important as having a uniquely useful garden. In fact, beauty is in and of itself very useful; beautification of a neighborhood can improve home value, bring a community together, feed people, attract businesses, and reduce crime. Cities and urban areas across the world are suffering from a challenging economic climate; we are suffering from economic strife in our cities, crime statistics are on the rise, and small towns are becoming ghost towns because there is no financial reason to live there. Beautiful gardens are needed because they create an emotional bond between people and their neighborhoods, keeping both businesses and neighbors actively involved and available within the community. While an area's physical landscaping and garden beauty might seem superficial, it is incredibly important as it presents opportunities for social activities and creates a feeling of neighborhood safety. Beautiful, colorful gardens bring community together.

Urban neighborhoods often have higher crime concerns, but studies focusing on green exposure have shown a surprising result. Scientists at the University of Illinois Urbana-Champaign's Landscape and Human Health Laboratory studied landscaping near public housing in Chicago. They discovered that areas beautified with flowers and plants have a reduced rate of home violence and residents have a more positive demeanor. These studies emphasize that beauty and greenery in a community will increase personal wellness and reduce crime. Understanding this can redefine how we focus on beauty and gardens within our neighborhood. By beautifying your home and community, you are building strong neighborhood ties that will lead to secure neighborhoods where the residents feel supported, cared about, and work together to protect one another.

Color in the Garden

Color in the garden is a personal choice. Whether you choose calming or exciting, color is a major player in the garden's visual appeal. This applies whether you are building a living wall or a traditional garden. A color wheel is made up of the

Formula Box

Colorful Foliage and Long-Blooming Flower Annuals for Partial Shade

- Beets, 'Bull's Blood'
- Begonia
- Caladium
- Coleus
- Dragon wing begonia
- Golden creeping jenny
- Kale
- Mondo grass
- New Guinea impatiens
- Polka dot plant
- Sweet potato vine
- Swiss chard
- Torenia

← A gorgeous living wall filled with color adds a lot to the garden; it draws the eye up, can be a source of food for the family, and brings beauty to a small area.

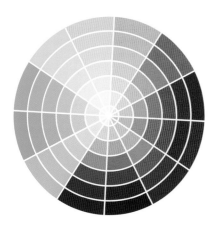

↑ A color wheel is a helpful tool when designing a colorful living wall.

Tools Needed

- 1 window box living wall system—purchased or built (See Resources, page 152)
- Hammer
- Screwdriver
- Containers
- Container soil
- Organic fertilizer
- Herbs and edible flowers

If hanging on wall:

- Drill
- Exterior lag screws and washers
- Socket wrench
- Tape measure
- Level

→ Plants used in this garden include begonia, coleus, dinosaur kale, dragonwing begonia, dusty miller, snapdragon, and sweet potato vine.

primary colors yellow, red, and blue. Secondary colors are purple, green, and orange. White and black are known as neutral colors.

There are several types of color schemes for the garden. Monochromatic, for example, could be an all-green theme like I originally had in my garden. It could mean all white—white flowers with white-leaved or silver-leaved plants. Perhaps you love yellow and would like a living wall that has all yellow flowering plants mixed with plants that have yellow on their foliage. Depending upon the color, monochromatic can be calming or stimulating. Monochromatic can also be amazingly eye catching. White is a neutral, yet it is easily seen at night. Therefore, if you are away from your house all day and spend more time in the garden in the evening, perhaps you would appreciate having white as a central, monochromatic theme because it stands out in the evening and early morning hours when you are more likely to be at home.

Complementary colors are opposing colors on the color wheel, such as yellow and purple. Building a garden that features yellow and purple together creates a stimulating color combination. There are many purple-foliaged plants available, so defining the colors as only coming from the flower aspect of the garden design is not necessary—use foliage for color as much as the flowers themselves. Orange and blue is another example of opposites. Blue foliage mixed with orange flowers is a bold statement.

Analogous colors are adjoining colors on the color wheel, such as the cooler colors of blue, purple, and red (or pink). They blend together more and create a harmonious garden view. Another example of adjoining color is the hot color combination of red, orange, and yellow. This color combination creates a stronger emphasis in the garden. Mixing colors in a creative way can improve your living wall design by giving the eye an interesting spot to rest and appreciate the view.

When creating a beautiful, color-filled wall, I have gone with the color combinations of green, blue, and red (or pink/burgundy in this case). "What?" you say, "That is madness! You're mixing up all the rules." Why, yes, I am! Rules are meant to be broken, and I love the foliage combinations of the sweet potato vine's chartreuse shades mixed with the blue colors of the kale mixed with the burgundy and pink found in the flowers in this gorgeous fence garden. Throwing in unexpected creativity is often what stimulates a beautiful garden. Use your best judgment when purchasing the seeds or plants. Start with a general color theme, then toss in a surprise to bring the beauty to a peak.

HOW TO BUILD A COLORFUL LIVING WALL

The system for hanging wall planters that's shown here is sturdy and easy to use and I like the way it looks. When you're choosing or making a window box living wall system, keep the convenience of being able to adjust the planter box height easily as your plants grow.

1. Set up the wall unit. Most come in two pieces that you secure with screws (provided).
2. If you're attaching the unit to a fence or wall, your best bet is to let it rest on the ground and simply drive a couple of deck screws through the top board and into the wall or fence. If you're hanging it so it is completely supported by the wall, use 3-inch exterior lag screws (with washers) driven through guide holes and into the wall—preferably at wall stud locations.
3. If using as a standalone floor unit, simply hammer on the special blocks that function as the feet of the unit.
4. Hang the wooden box frames onto the wood back supports by hooking them on as shown in the manufacturer's directions.
5. Turn over the plastic containers that come with the unit and punch out the drainage holes with a screwdriver.
6. Mix container soil with organic fertilizer and fill soil in the unit (see pages 32 to 34).
7. Plant your plants tightly into the plastic garden containers, then drop the containers into the wooden frames.
8. Water well.

↑ Assemble the back of the living wall. It is used to hold the planting box–style soil containers tightly against the fence or wall.

↑ When the back portion of the living wall is screwed to the wall or fence, it will be flat and ready for the planting boxes.

↑ Hang the planting boxes in the design configuration you choose—there is no right or wrong.

↑ Punch out the drainage holes in the planting boxes and fill with the appropriate soil mix.

↑ Once planted, maintain with regular watering and organic fertilizing throughout the season.

VITAMIN-RICH CULINARY GARDEN

Fresh Herbs and Vegetables at Your Fingertips

WHAT DO YOU DO when you live and work in a heavily urban or industrialized area and you want to have fresh, organic vegetables for your family? Grow them, of course. The garden featured in this project is shown at an industrial nursery. Families that work there are encouraged to share and use the fruits, herbs, and vegetables by taking the vegetables home to family or by eating them at their lunch hour.

Getting your family to eat vegetables might be a battle reminiscent of Godzilla, but there's a surprisingly successful approach that can get them to try vegetables and like them: have them grow their own! Fresh vegetables ripened in the garden typically taste better than vegetables that are grown far away, picked while in a still green state, then left to ripen on the shelf. The fruits and vegetables you find in the grocery might look ripe, but the way they have ripened means less taste and nutrition.

Vegetables that are shelf ripened also look different than vegetables that are home grown. When you grow your own vegetables and pick them at the peak of ripeness you discover a vegetable that has rich colors, strong tastes, and a sweetness that can be overwhelming. This is the way to get the family to fall in love with vegetables; having a vegetable that is at the top of its taste and color is appealing and will get consumed, but having a vegetable that looks and tastes bland is not appealing to young palates.

Children Like to Grow

Kids like to garden for a number of reasons. There is nothing better than getting messy by planting seeds or vegetables in a big pile of dirt. Planting is fun. Watching a child's face light up when they finally understand that a tiny seed is going to grow into a cucumber or some other edible wonder is an amazing process. By teaching your kids to garden, you are teaching them the entire circle of life. They learn that growth does not happen without nurturing and that it is each human's responsibility to help nurture one another through life.

When your family grows together, they water and watch the plants develop together as well. It is a home-community building process that can last an entire season, sometimes over three seasons of growth. Each time your family comes together to nurture a garden, you are contributing to positive mental health by reducing stress and calming your minds. Physical health benefits include increased oxygen exposure and, of course, exposure to the natural world in general. Growing a plant yourself means you get to reap the rewards: tasting the vegetables. This is truly the best way to get someone hooked on fresh food. Once you try a ripe, freshly picked vegetable, it is all you will crave

Formula Box

High-Vitamin Content Vegetables and Herbs

- Arugula
- Beets, 'Bull's Blood'
- Bell peppers
- Broccoli
- Carrots
- Chinese cabbage
- Cilantro
- Collard greens
- Kale
- Lima beans
- Mustard greens
- Oregano
- Parsley
- Peas
- Rosemary
- Spinach
- Sweet potato
- Swiss chard
- Watercress

← Living walls come in many shapes and forms and are most needed in urban communities where there is very little growing space. Seeing a living wall vegetable garden growing in an industrial area is reason for celebration.

Vitamin Sources

- Potassium: beans, potatoes, winter squash, greens of all sorts
- Folate: beans, green peas, peanuts, dark-green leafy vegetables
- Vitamin A: orange vegetables such as pumpkin, sweet potatoes, and carrots; tomatoes; dark-green leafy vegetables such as turnip greens, collards, and spinach
- Vitamin B6: broccoli, cauliflower, peas, potatoes, red bell pepper, and spinach
- Vitamin C: fruits such as cantaloupe and strawberries; broccoli; tomatoes; cabbage; potatoes; peppers; and leafy greens such as turnip greens, spinach, and romaine lettuce

↑ While it is best to use smaller leafy plants in a living wall garden such as this one, large plants can still find their place as is seen with these collard greens.

in the future. When children are able to pick the vegetables that they grew themselves, you are helping them form a connection between growing and their own mental and physical health.

Where the Vitamins Are

Growing a vitamin-rich culinary garden is as simple as making your living wall vegetable garden as colorful as you possibly can. A basic rule related to vitamin content and vegetables is this: more color equals more vitamins. Bold-colored Swiss chard, orange carrots, deep-green spinach, and red 'Bull's Blood' beets are full of color and nutrients, which include phytochemicals and antioxidants. Consuming lots of color and a variety of fresh vegetables and fruits will help you have a most well-balanced diet.

Herbs are also powerful vitamin machines when consumed. One teaspoon of thyme can provide 20 percent of your daily iron requirements. Cilantro, particularly the seed, is known to improve cardiovascular health. Oregano has more cancer-fighting antioxidants than blueberries. Using fresh herbs and vegetables in your everyday cooking schedule will enhance your family's diet.

There are many types of vitamins in vegetables, and some vegetables are known as "powerhouses" because of the large quantity of nutrients in one plant. Therefore, you might choose to grow a vegetable or plant that provides a nutrient you know you and your family might not be getting enough of. This could stimulate more interest in that particular vegetable, particularly if you grow it and like it, so you will continue to consume the vegetable in the future. Growing a variety of colorful vegetables will give you a well-rounded, vitamin-rich diet. Whether you grow at work or at home with your family, be sure to taste the amazing flavor that can be discovered with high-vitamin vegetables.

A VITAMIN-RICH CULINARY GARDEN

1. Assemble or build your living wall unit.
2. If you're attaching the unit to a fence or wall, your best bet is to let it rest just above the ground and simply drive a couple of deck screws through the top board and into the wall or fence. If you're hanging it so it is completely supported by the wall, use 3-inch exterior lag screws (with washers) driven through guide holes and into the wall—preferably at wall stud locations.
3. If using as a standalone floor unit, simply hammer on the special blocks that function as the feet of the unit, if your system can be freestanding.
4. Hang the wooden box frames onto the wood back supports by hooking them on as shown in the manufacturer's directions.
5. Turn over the plastic containers that come with the unit and punch out the drainage holes with a screwdriver.
6. Mix container soil with organic fertilizer and fill soil in the unit (see pages 32 to 34).
7. Plant your veggies tightly into the plastic garden containers, then drop the containers into the wooden frames.
8. Water well.

↑ Assemble the unit. Because this is a freestanding unit that is not attached to the wall, the "feet" of the unit must be hammered on before the rest of the garden can be assembled.

↑ Punch holes in the bottom of the planting boxes and arrange them on the living wall.

↑ Fill with an organic soil mix, leaving about an inch of space at the top of the soil level.

→ Assemble the garden with whichever plants you prefer. This garden has a mixture of herb and vegetables, including basil, oregano, collard greens, parsley, Swiss chard, and kale.

URBAN WATER-SAVING GARDEN

Conserve Water and Make a Difference

SAVING MONEY BY PLANTING with seeds or reusing garden planting systems is a great way to grow frugally. Water, however, is one of the biggest gardening expenses around the world. By learning to save water, you are learning to save money. Living walls, if used properly, can save water and expense.

Humans are wasting water. In the United States alone, it is estimated that more than one trillion gallons of water are wasted annually nationwide. For the average household, this means that water leaks can account for an astounding waste of 10,000 gallons of water annually. Irrigation systems are often installed to water grass, which is a nonfood-producing, nonpollinator-supporting crop with heavy water requirements. Lawn watering consumes over 30 percent of the water used on the East Coast of the United States during the spring and summer seasons. Many of these irrigation systems leak, which means that a slow leak about the thickness of a $\frac{1}{32}$ of an inch can waste over 6,300 gallons of water per month.

World Drought

Drought is currently a pervasive environmental concern for most of the world. Extreme weather and climactic events are a natural part of Earth's system. Yet drought and heat waves are particularly challenging for the act of gardening, having significant impacts on our community and lives. According to the Intergovernmental Panel on Climate Change, "confidence has increased that some weather events and extremes will become more frequent, more widespread or more intense during the 21st century." In other words, look out for more of the same in future years.

In areas such as Southern California, South Africa, Spain, and other European regions, severe drought has been devastating to crops, having a severe socioeconomic effect on communities as well. In these regions, saving water is not a considerate thing to do; it's an absolute necessity.

Watering Your Living Wall Garden

Living wall gardens can be quite water-saving efficient because gardens of this nature are typically hand watered or have automatic watering as a part of their growing systems. Sprinklers waste tons of water annually, so the advantage of living walls is that they lose less water through evaporation of the watering process. Using a watering wand when watering, instead of spraying directly with a hose, is a great step toward saving water. Utilizing an automated irrigation system is perhaps the best way to save water, but irrigation is not always available to a gardener.

Formula Box

Drought-Tolerant Herbs and Vegetables

- Amaranth
- Broccoli
- Chamomile, German
- Chards
- Chinese cabbage
- Lavender
- Malabar spinach
- Oregano
- Peppers
- Rhubarb
- Sage
- Thyme
- Tomatoes
- Winter Savory

← Growing in regions of the country that suffer drought often means there is a lot of brown in the scenery. Why not perk up a dry, hot area with bold color, both in plantings and in container and wall design? This living wall shelf is a fantastic way to bring color to a dull area.

It is possible to take the concept of saving water through living walls to the next level by carefully planning the container system. A self-watering container helps save water by allowing you to water less over a period of time. For example, a self-watering unit such as an EarthBox gardening system holds more water than a traditional container within a reservoir hidden at the base of the planting container. This water is then absorbed slowly by the plant roots and requires less watering than the typical container or wall unit, thereby saving water for you and your family.

EarthBox gardening systems come in several varieties, most commonly regular sized or junior sized. While large EarthBox gardening systems function well for big plants such as tomato or eggplant, it is quite possible to use an EarthBox Junior gardening system for a small patio living wall. Build a shelf system unit and water the plants through the water tube. Depending on air humidity, you may only have to water once or twice per week.

Using Less Water

If you can combine the conceptual idea of watering less with the principle of growing plants that can tolerate higher temperatures and require less water, you have created a double layer of defense against drought conditions. Traditional plants need less water when they are planted in a richer soil that absorbs moisture. There are several soil mixes mentioned on page 33, and using a mix that has traditional potting soil mixed with compost, worm castings, and other natural ingredients increases its water-holding capacity immensely. Succulents or cactus are also strongly drought tolerant but require heavier drainage.

Planting vegetables closer together actually helps conserve water. Each plant can shade and help preserve the other plant, and they share water this way. In this fashion, living walls, by their nature, are water saving because they grow plants in close quarters.

If you are not using an EarthBox garden system, your living wall should be watered at the base of your plants in the evening or at night. This ensures the plant will hold more water for a longer period of time. Only switch to morning watering if the living wall shows signs of powdery mildew or fungus. If the living wall does not have an automated or self-watering system, it is best to water for a longer period of time fewer times during the week. If the system is automated or a self-watering system like the EarthBox gardening systems, simply water the containers according to system directions.

Plants with silver or white leaves, such as artemesia or dusty miller are often drought tolerant. Flowering plants such as amaranth, cleome, Diamond Frost Euphorbia, lantana, oxalis, and verbena are quite drought tolerant. Herbs that are drought tolerant can frequently be found in Mediterranean recipes: rosemary, oregano, and sage are wonderfully hardy. Vegetables include cool-season growers such as cabbage, kale, and chards. Summer-season growers that do remarkably well with little water include peppers, tomatoes, and broccoli.

AN URBAN WATER-SAVING GARDEN

❶ Measure the wall that will hold the self-watering planters for customized shelf placement.

❷ Cut the wood to size if necessary.

❸ Nail the 62-inch side pieces to the top and bottom of the 28-inch 1 × 10s.

❹ Place the remaining 28-inch 1 × 10s at 17⅝-inch intervals, nailing through the outside of the 62-inch board to hold the shelf in place.

❺ Nail the 2 × 4 boards on the bottom of the unit.

❻ Nail the 1 × 4 boards cut to 9¼ inches to the sides of the unit at the top and bottom to form a rim trim.

❼ Nail the 1 × 4 boards cut to 29 inches to the front of the unit at the top and bottom to connect the trim.

❽ Top the unit with the one 1 × 10 board cut to 30 inches.

❾ Attach heavy-duty hanging hooks on the back of the unit. Use the level to be sure both hooks are level for hanging.

❿ Paint or stain.

⓫ Using two heavy-duty nails, hammer nails into the wall, check for level, then hang the unit.

⓬ If using the EarthBox Junior gardening systems, follow the directions to plant using the enclosed fertilizer and planting tray cover—assemble, fill with soil, add organic fertilizer, cut holes in the cover, and plant the garden.

⓭ If using a different self-watering container, follow the directions as required.

Gather all the materials for planting: unit, soil, trowel, and plants. This living wall has basil, dusty miller, red salvia, rosemary, and sweet potato vine.

Build a Custom Shelf

- 2 1 × 10-inch boards cut to 62 inches
- 4 1 × 10-inch boards cut to 28 inches
- 2 2 × 4-foot boards cut to 28 inches
- 4 1 × 4-inch boards cut to 9¼ inches
- 2 1 × 4-inch boards cut to 29 inches
- 1 1 × 10-inch board cut to 30 inches

Design by Ricky Rolon
Illustration by Bill Kersey

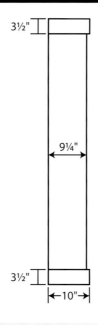

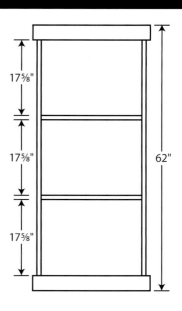

↑ Begin by laying out the supplies needed to build the shelf. Level and measure twice to make sure your project will work well.

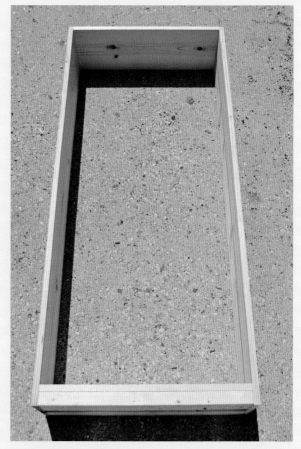

↑ Assemble the frame of the garden shelf.

↑ Nail the shelves into place.

↑ Attach decorative trim and paint the front of the unit.

↑ Attach heavy-duty hooks to hang the unit without additional support.

↑ Pull out the water-saving planter kit while the paint is drying and review the instructions.

↑ Add organic soil amendments to the soil, then plant the plants accordingly. Follow the planter directions as indicated.

↑ Water-saving planters conserve water because of their bottom-up watering technique that keeps roots cool and moist longer.

LIVING WALL MAINTENANCE

LIKE ALL GARDENS, living walls need regular maintenance. While they save enormous amounts of time because they do not require weeding and can grow a lot more plants in a small space, they also need regular tender, loving care to maintain their beauty. Consistent maintenance is truly the difference between a dead garden and lasting living wall.

There are many different varieties of living wall systems right within this book that you might be able to use for your own garden. Planning for the garden's maintenance might better enable you to choose the right system and the right plants for your vertical garden experience. Maintenance of the living wall system you choose is divided into two categories: growing maintenance and fall maintenance.

Tip

RECIPE FOR HOMEMADE 2-PERCENT INSECTICIDE SOAP

- Large batch:
  5 tablespoons all-natural castile soap to 1 gallon of water

- Small batch:
  1 heaping tablespoon of all-natural castile soap to 1 quart of water

Mix the ingredients together, making sure the soap is dissolved in the water, then fill a sprayer with the mixture. Spray the insects directly, as spraying the plant is not sufficient. Soap clogs the insects' pores, so most will die when directly sprayed.

Growing Maintenance

Of course, the most obvious and consistent maintenance required after planting a living wall is regular watering. Whether you hand water or have a water system installed, each requires that you regularly check on the living wall to make sure it is receiving the water it requires. With an efficient irrigation system, you can certainly make your living wall far more self-sustaining.

Living walls all require trimming and pruning upon occasion. Remove dead, diseased, or weak leaves and use your hand pruners to trim down overgrown areas as needed. Plants take time to grow, so pay attention as they grow in. If you have a plant that does not adapt well, browns out, or even dies, you should remove that plant and replace it with a substitute that works.

Should the plants you have installed consistently show signs of a severe disease, such as a blight or fungus, treat organically whenever possible and double-check that you are growing the right plants for the right conditions. Regular applications of organic fertilizer should be applied as needed throughout the season either in water soluble form or as a top dressing to soiled systems.

Fall Maintenance

Although some gardeners around the world are able to keep both their traditional and their living walls up year-round, the vast majority of gardeners close down or slow down their garden in the late fall and winter. Some people prefer to pull all the plants and soil out of the living walls and store the living wall inside for the winter. Others prefer to leave the unit outside attached to the fence or wall while only cleaning out the plants and soil until it is replanting time in the spring.

Eventually, even in the warm tropical regions of the world where the plants continue to grow year-round, the living wall will have to have its soil or root zone replenished with nutrients and will have to be checked for root problems. This is usually done in the fall every one to two years. Take all the plants out, divide or remove those plants that are rootbound, pull the soil out, replace the soil with freshly amended soil, and replant the plants.

Pests

Living walls attract butterflies, bees, and many flying insects and rarely attract snails or other pests that are known to primarily be ground invaders. Mother Nature has a beautiful way of developing a balance in the garden, particularly in relationship to bugs and other pests. Quite often, when you have too many buggy pests on a living wall, birds come along and eat all the pests. Birds can also be the pests themselves and eat or attack berries you might be growing. Then the solution is to temporarily net the living wall until the berries are done ripening.

For every pest there is a good creature that needs to eat dinner. That dinner is the bad bug. Sounds harsh, doesn't it? Yet there have been many times in my garden that I have simply waited out a pest problem and another good bug or animal came along to solve it for me. If I have a few flowers and their leaves are eaten through or looking a bit rough, it is balanced by the fact that my vegetables might not have any pests on them because they are all hanging out on those flowers. In fact, I often grow companion plants specifically with that in mind.

Companion Planting

Companion planting is based on the concept of growing specific plants close to each other so that you can attract beneficial insects or repel pest-like insects. You can easily grow companion plants together within our living wall system if you are concerned about certain pests being a problem.

Attracting beneficial insects might help keep those bad insects in check. While companion planting does not guarantee pest-free production, it can certainly help in reducing the pesky issues. "Trap cropping" is a term that defines the conceptual idea of attracting an insect to a crop, letting it suffer a lot of damage by the insect, in hopes that the insect will never touch the nontrap crops. This sacrificial system works well in my experience.

Trap cropping can work in two ways:

Plant a lot of the same plant. For example, if you are growing a microliving wall farm in an urban situation, you plant an entire wall of cabbage instead of just a few cabbages in the hope that the cabbage moth caterpillar might attack and consume only a few of the plants instead of all of them. This is usually most effective when the trap crop is planted much earlier than the primary crop so that the pest hits the first crop and stays with it for the duration of the season.

Plant an entirely different species of plant. For example, you might plant cilantro beside your cabbage plants in order to attract parasitic wasps, which will hopefully attack the cabbage moth caterpillar.

Compost and Worm Castings

While it is possible to purchase compost and worm castings, you can also make these ingredients yourself, depending on how much room you have, and save a tremendous amount of money. Worm compost bins fit well in apartment or condominium living conditions as they are kept indoors. Worms thrive best in temperatures that range between 50° and 75° Fahrenheit. Temperatures can be extremely hot in the summer and extremely cold in the winter, so having a kitchen composter or closet composter in a small living unit in an urban area can make a lot of sense.

Of course, you can leave the bins outside if the weather is mild, but this is risky as you never know when you might receive a sweltering day or a frost

↑ You can build a stacking bin for vermicomposting from wood if you have the carpentry skills, or you can find many easy plans online for making one from a plastic tub. *Cool Springs Press*

↑ The stacking trays are filled with shredded newspaper, dirt, and kitchen scraps. You rotate them in much the same way as you would in a multi-bin composting bin. *Cool Springs Press*

↑ Harvested worm castings lend a wide spectrum of nutrients to your living wall garden. *Crystal Liepa Photography*

↑ You'll find thousands of plans online for building your own compost bin. Choose one that fits nicely into your garden design. *Cool Springs Press*

during the night. Worms are fun—they can also be greatly rewarding when you purchase or build your own bin and make castings for your living wall.

HOW TO MAKE WORM CASTINGS

- Obtain a commercially sold worm bin or make your own. Try to find a local source for *Eugenia fetid* worms, the type commonly sold for worm bins. You will have the most success with this variety.

- Mail-order travel can shake the worms up, so they might act strangely and try to escape the worm bin upon arrival. Local worms often are raised in standard worm containers already and are not as traumatized by a move. Long-distance shipping seems to have a more profound effect on the worms, but if long distance is the only way you can receive worms, you will have to go that route.

- Worms are normally sold by the pound. Start with one pound. The more compost you have, the more worms you will need, but be cautious about ordering too many worms. You can determine if you need additional worms once you start composting and see how much kitchen waste you regularly produce for the worms to consume.

- Prepare the bin by shredding plain black and white newspaper into narrow strips. Paper shredders are great for this. Soak bare cardboard (without printing or inks) in water, then tear it into four- to five-inch-square pieces and place the pieces in the bin. Moisten the newspaper strips until damp but not sodden and place them in the bin with the cardboard. Be sure to wring the strips out thoroughly—there should be no standing water in the worm bin. Layer the newspaper about 6 inches deep.

- Add 2 cups of organic soil or compost to the mix to help with the worms' digestion. Toss everything together like a salad, then add the new worms and cover them with a bit of the paper so they are not exposed to light.

- Start feeding the worms slowly. If you overfeed your worms, your bin can become smelly. Place 1 cup of kitchen scraps in a corner of the bin and cover it with the newspapers. Worms like softer foods and smaller chunks rather than large, hard food.

- After several days, check on the worms and add another cup of scraps. Keep this process up every few days.

Feed the worms shredded newspaper, paper egg cartons, wet bread and pasta, fruit (no citrus), lettuce and other vegetables (such as squash, fresh or cooked), crushed eggshells, tea leaves, dry leaves, and coffee grounds. Do not use citrus, dairy, meat, oil, pre-packaged foods, salty food, vinegar, or sugar. These items will trigger an imbalance in the worm bin system and make it smelly since worms cannot digest them properly.

Ultimately the worms will eat everything in the bin—all the paper and food scraps will be condensed into worm poop, or worm castings. This is garden gold for the living wall systems that require soil. Worm castings do not smell or have an odor beyond that of soil and are powerfully water retentive, so they make a perfect soil additive.

HOW TO MAKE TRADITIONAL COMPOST

Making traditional compost is easy, but it does require a larger outdoor area than a worm bin, so is better for homeowners, community gardens and allotment areas, or shared apartment and condominium areas that allow composting. Much like worm composting, making compost is very easy and saves a lot of money because it is the best way to create absolutely free nutrient-rich humus for your living wall and garden.

There are many amazing reasons to use compost; it is remarkably good for the environment because it recycles yard and kitchen waste and keeps it out of landfills. Compost is filled with microscopic organisms that are incredibly wonderful for your plants' root systems. Soils that have heavy compost content are also able to retain moisture for a longer period of time. While organic compost does not have a heavy level of nitrogen, it is strong enough that it can significantly reduce the need to use chemical fertilizers.

To begin composting, you need a place to compost, such as a composting bin or a composting pile area. There needs to be a consistent mix of nitrogen-rich materials, "greens"; carbon-rich materials, "browns"; and moisture. Below is a list of browns and greens that make excellent ingredients in your compost pile. Never use meat or bones, as they can cause your pile to smell and attract vermin. Never use dog, human, or cat manure/feces, as they can contain pathogens or diseases that could be harmful.

↑ Most building centers and garden stores sell many styles of compost bins for making your own living wall garden soil. *pryzmat/Shutterstock*

Examples of browns
- Aged grass clippings
- Brown paper bags and shredded cardboard
- Newspaper (black-and-white soy print is best)
- Shredded cotton and paper-based tissues and towels
- Dryer lint
- Straw
- Dead shredded leaves from healthy plants (do not use diseased plants)

Examples of greens
- Coffee grounds
- Barnyard animal manures, such as llama, cow, horse, goat, chicken, sheep, and rabbit
- New grass clippings
- Pulled weeds and plant prunings (do not add prunings from diseased plants)
- Tea bags with metal staple and string removed
- Kitchen scraps (avoid items that will root, such as potato skins and onions, unless they are ground completely)
- Eggshells
- Fresh flower cuttings
- Seaweed and/or kelp

Composting seems to work best when the ingredients are exposed to the ground. Place a few layers of sticks or straw on the bottom of the bin to leave an airy drainage area. Start layering compost materials, mixing a brown layer and a green layer, and then repeat this process over time. Heavy nitrogen items such as green manure—grass clippings, clover, wheatgrass, or any heavy nitrogen source—will stimulate the composting process.

Speedier composting happens with good balance of carbon and nitrogen and turning the pile regularly, either with a pitchfork, compost crank, or another turning tool. Turn every few weeks. On average, it takes between three and four weeks to make your own compost. It's good if your pile is hot to the touch, because it indicates a heavier activity level in the decomposition process. To increase activity, add even more green materials and place your composter in full sun. Additionally, keep the pile moist, but not soggy. Organic waste needs water to decompose. The rule of thumb is to keep your compost pile as wet as a wrung-out sponge.

ONLINE PRODUCT RESOURCES

Part I

(pages 21 to 39)

Potting Scoop With Cutter by DeWit or "The Shawna Trowel"	www.dewittoolsusa.com/dutch-hand-tools
CobraHead Weeder and Cultivator	www.cobrahead.com/categories
Dramm ColorPoint Bypass Pruner	www.rainwand.com/cutting.html
Dramm One Touch Rain Wand	www.rainwand.com/one-touch.html
Le Jardinet Garden Dibbers and Row Markers	www.lejardinetdesigns.com/garden-dibber
The Seedkeeper Seed Storage Unit	www.seedkeepercompany.com
Organic Mechanics Soil and Worm Castings	www.organicmechanicsoil.com
Authentic Haven Brand Soil Conditional Tea "Moo Poo Tea"	www.ahavenbrand.com

Part II

(pages 41 to 151)

Felt Wrap Living Wall Systems

Florafelt Compact Kit	www.florafelt.com

Hydroponic Soilless Systems

Sagewall system	www.sageverticalgardens.com

Window Box Living Wall Systems

Gro Products Vertical Growing System	www.groproducts.com
Gronomic Vertical Garden Bed System	www.gronomics.com
GroVert Living Wall Planter Kit	www.brightgreenusa.com

Planting Pocket Systems

Woolly Pocket Wally Garden Wall Pockets	www.woollypocket.com

Bracket-Hung Framed Art Walls

GroVert Living Wall Planter Kit	www.brightgreenusa.com

Modular Planter and Bracket System

Living Wall Planter	www.woollypocket.com
Compoclay Living Wall Planter	www.compoclay.com

CONTRIBUTORS

Herbal Cocktail Garden

| Gro Products Vertical Growing System | www.groproducts.com |
| Plants—Jung Seed Co. | www.jungseed.com |

Moss and Shade Wall Art

| Metal Art Sculpture | www.regalgift.com |
| Plants—Moss and Stone Gardens | www.mossandstonegardens.com |

Vegetable "Balconies" Garden

| Gro Products Vertical Growing System | www.groproducts.com |
| Plants—Jung Seed Co. | www.jungseed.com |

Fern Garden

| Windswept Cone—Tierra Garden | www.tierragarden.com |
| Plants—The Planter's Palette | www.planterspalette.com |

Cactus Living Wall

| Gardener's Supply Company Copper Vertical Wall Garden | www.gardeners.com |
| Plants—Schaefer Greenhouses Inc. | www.schaefergreenhouses.com |

Therapeutic Hanging Gardens

Vintage Jardin Jars	www.syndicatesales.com
Plants—Jung Seed Co.	www.jungseed.com
Mini Woolly Pocket Wally Garden Wall Pockets	www.woollypocket.com
Large black jack chain and hardware	local hardware store

Hydroponic Pollinator Garden

| Sagewall system | www.sageverticalgardens.com |
| Plants—The Planter's Palette | www.planterspalette.com |

Shade Pallet Garden

| Plants—Jung Seed Co. | www.jungseed.com |

Insulate-a-Wall Garden

| Compoclay Living Wall Planter | www.compoclay.com |
| Plants—The Planter's Palette | www.planterspalette.com |

Bookshelf Fence Garden

| Galvanized tin metal planters | www.syndicatesales.com |
| Plants—Jung Seed Co. | www.jungseed.com |

Succulent Living Wall

| Gardener's Supply Company Copper Vertical Wall Garden | www.gardeners.com |
| Plants—The Planter's Palette | www.planterspalette.com |

Vertical Vegetable Farm

| Gronomic Vertical Garden Bed System | www.gronomics.com |
| Plants—Jung Seed Co. | www.jungseed.com |

Aphrodisiac Wall Garden

| Compoclay Living Wall Planter | www.compoclay.com |
| Plants—Jung Seed Co. | www.jungseed.com |

Freestanding Entrance Garden

| Florafelt Compact Kit | www.florafelt.com |
| Plants—Optimara | www.optimara.com |

Culinary Kitchen Garden

| Woolly Pocket Wally Garden Wall Pockets | www.woollypocket.com |
| Plants—The Planter's Palette | www.planterspalette.com |

Aromatherapy Garden

| Bright Green GroVert Living Wall Planter Kit | www.brightgreenusa.com |
| Plants—Schaefer Greenhouses Inc. | www.schaefergreenhouses.com |

Money-Saving Garden

| Living Wall Planter | www.woollypocket.com |
| Plants—The Planter's Palette | www.planterspalette.com |

Smart Garden

| Bright Green GroVert Living Wall Planter Kit | www.brightgreenusa.com |
| Plants—Schaefer Greenhouses Inc. | www.schaefergreenhouses.com |

Colorful Living Wall

| Gro Products Vertical Growing System | www.groproducts.com |
| Plants—Jung Seed Co. | www.jungseed.com |

Vitamin-Rich Culinary Garden

| Gro Products Vertical Growing System | www.groproducts.com |
| Plants—Schaefer Greenhouses Inc. | www.schaefergreenhouses.com |

Urban Water-Saving Garden

| EarthBox Junior Gardening System | earthbox.com |
| Plants—Jung Seed Co. | www.jungseed.com |

ACKNOWLEDGMENTS

BOOKS CANNOT BE WRITTEN alone; there are so very many people that either helped contribute or helped inspire the completion of this book. Thanks one and all for all your support, particularly my editor Mark Johanson and all the staff at Cool Springs Press who truly believed in me and my goals for the book from the very beginning. Your saint-like patience in dealing with my quirky mindset and driven work routine goes way above and beyond the call of duty.

I have the coolest family ever, and they support me while I'm locked in my office typing thousands of words—thanks to Luis and my daughters for helping me get'er done while inspiring me to keep focused on what is really important in life.

Thank you to all of the viewers of my blog, newspaper column, and videos. Your faithful support has been what has cheered me on to find a way to connect the world with the conceptual idea of making a difference.

Rockin' Ricky Rolon is my carpenter and good friend—he's responsible for helping me build and assemble nearly all the living wall projects in this book. You are marvelous, Ricky. Thanks for helping me, bro! The Dirty Glove Society has held my hand through all the challenges of growing over 2,000 plants while writing this book and simultaneously trying to manage my family life, a consulting business, a speaking tour schedule, and blogging commitments. Your ever-present friendship encourages me to get it all done with a minimum of insanity. This season I had several garden helpers who helped me weed and mulch in my primary garden so that I could work nonstop on the keyboard. Thanks to Lori Ammons, Steve Deangeles, Sammi Garon, Bek Lieto, René Silinis, and many other friends and helpers who randomly showed up with dirty pants on, gloves in hand, and a giant smile on their faces to work in the garden.

There were many expeditions to the Chicago Botanic Garden, Ball Horticultural, and countless other gardens to take photos of astounding living walls. Helen Yoest was kind enough to allow me to feature an aphrodisiac garden based on her book concept. Then there were the spectacular friends from various companies that allowed me to use their plants and products in this book—Authentic Haven Brand Moo Poo Tea, CobraHead, Dewit Tools, Dramm, Earthbox, Le Jardinet, Organic Mechanics Soil, Syndicate Sales, The Seedkeeper Company, and Tierra Garden. And, of course, thanks to the living wall system companies—Bright Green, Compoclay, Florafelt, Gardeners.com, Gronomics, Gro Products, and Woolly Pocket.

Thanks to Russell from Optimara for the incredible tropical plants. David Spain from Moss and Stone Gardens sent his remarkably cool moss and gave me personal lessons on how to grow it. Diana Stoll, David Tyznyk, and Greg Milauskas at The Planter's Palette allowed me to plant and hang a half-dozen wall systems with their gorgeous plants at the garden center. Thank you all for your inspiration and friendship. Bret Schaeffer from Schaeffer's Greenhouse also deserves thanks for allowing me to grow several living wall systems at his garden center. Finally, I give my deep heartfelt thanks to Jung Seed Co. and the Zondag family who provided me with hundreds of plants for the majority of the living wall system plantings—your plants were awesome and beautiful and perfectly wonderful in every way. Thank you all for believing in me and working with me.

CONVERSIONS

Metric Equivalent

Inches (in.)	1/64	1/32	1/25	1/16	1/8	1/4	3/8	2/5	1/2	5/8	3/4	7/8	1	2	3	4	5	6	7	8	9	10	11	12	36	39.4
Feet (ft.)																								1	3	3 1/12
Yards (yd.)																									1	1 1/12
Millimeters (mm)	0.40	0.79	1	1.59	3.18	6.35	9.53	10	12.7	15.9	19.1	22.2	25.4	50.8	76.2	101.6	127	152	178	203	229	254	279	305	914	1,000
Centimeters (cm)							0.95	1	1.27	1.59	1.91	2.22	2.54	5.08	7.62	10.16	12.7	15.2	17.8	20.3	22.9	25.4	27.9	30.5	91.4	100
Meters (m)																								.30	.91	1.00

Converting Measurements

To Convert:	To:	Multiply by:
Inches	Millimeters	25.4
Inches	Centimeters	2.54
Feet	Meters	0.305
Yards	Meters	0.914
Miles	Kilometers	1.609
Square inches	Square centimeters	6.45
Square feet	Square meters	0.093
Square yards	Square meters	0.836
Cubic inches	Cubic centimeters	16.4
Cubic feet	Cubic meters	0.0283
Cubic yards	Cubic meters	0.765
Pints (U.S.)	Liters	0.473 (Imp. 0.568)
Quarts (U.S.)	Liters	0.946 (Imp. 1.136)
Gallons (U.S.)	Liters	3.785 (Imp. 4.546)
Ounces	Grams	28.4
Pounds	Kilograms	0.454
Tons	Metric tons	0.907

To Convert:	To:	Multiply by:
Millimeters	Inches	0.039
Centimeters	Inches	0.394
Meters	Feet	3.28
Meters	Yards	1.09
Kilometers	Miles	0.621
Square centimeters	Square inches	0.155
Square meters	Square feet	10.8
Square meters	Square yards	1.2
Cubic centimeters	Cubic inches	0.061
Cubic meters	Cubic feet	35.3
Cubic meters	Cubic yards	1.31
Liters	Pints (U.S.)	2.114 (Imp. 1.76)
Liters	Quarts (U.S.)	1.057 (Imp. 0.88)
Liters	Gallons (U.S.)	0.264 (Imp. 0.22)
Grams	Ounces	0.035
Kilograms	Pounds	2.2
Metric tons	Tons	1.1

Converting Temperatures

Convert degrees Fahrenheit (F) to degrees Celsius (C) by following this simple formula:

Subtract 32 from the Fahrenheit temperature reading. Then mulitply that number by 5/9.
For example, 77°F – 32 = 45. 45 × 5/9 = 25°C.

To convert degrees Celsius to degrees Fahrenheit, multiply the Celsius temperature reading by 9/5, then add 32.
For example, 25°C × 9/5 = 45. 45 + 32 = 77°F.

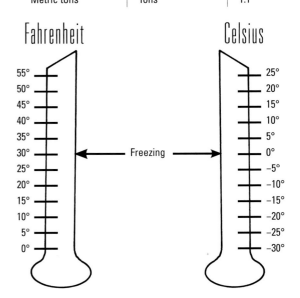

INDEX

Projects appear in bold face.
Page numbers in italics indicate
a photograph or caption.

acrocarpous moss, 47–49
aesthetics, 135–136. *See also* design
ageratum, 73
air plants, 11
air pollution, 51
air quality, 13, 51–52, 107–108,
    131
alcohol infusions, 43–44
Aloe vera, 93, 107
alyssum, 73, 125
amaranth, 143–144
angelonia, 73
anise hyssop, 39, 119
annuals, 36-37. *See also*
    flowers; vegetables
aphrodisiacs, 101–102
Aphrodisiac Wall Garden, 101–105
aromatherapy, 119–121
Aromatherapy Garden, 119–123
arrowhead vine, 131
artemesia, 119, 144
arugula, 39, 51–52, 97, 139
asbestos, 90
Associated Landscape Contractors of
    America (ALCA), 108, 131
attention restoration theory, 131
attention span, 131–133
automated irrigation systems, 31, 99,
    109–111, 143

bag systems, 23. *See also* loose-medium
    systems
Ball Horticultural Company, *10, 18*
basil
    for aphrodisiac garden, 101, 102
    for aromatherapy gardens, 119
    as cocktail herb, 43
    for culinary gardens, 113
    globe, 39, 65
    as ornamental plant, 38–39
    as oxygenator, 51–52
    as part-shade plant, 89
    'Pesto Perpetuo', 39
    purple, 83
    small-space gardening and, 97
    'Thai', 39
    for therapeutic gardens, 65
beans, 125
bees, 7–8, 36, 73–74

beets
    for aphrodisiac garden, 101
    'Bull's Blood', 37, 39, 83, 135, 139
    greens, 52
    as ornamental plants, 38–39, 135
    from seed, 125
    small-space gardening and, 97
    vitamin content of, 139
begonias
    for color, *18*, 135
    dragon wing, 135
    'Gryphon', 79
    as part-shade plant, 89, 135
biowalls. *See* living walls
bisphenol A (BPA), 31
block systems, 22, 23
bloodmeal, *34*
bok choy, 52
bolting, 44, 97
Bookshelf Fence Garden, 89–91
broccoli, 102, 139, 143–144
Brookfield Zoo, *16*
burro's tail, 93
butterflies, 8, 73. *See also* pollinators
bypass pruners, 27

cabbage
    as aphrodisiac, 102
    Chinese, 139, 143
    as ornamental plant, 38, 39
    as oxygenator, 51–52
cactus
    about, 59
    edible, 60–61
    handling, *59, 61, 62*
    soil for, 33
    watering needs, 31
Cactus Living Wall, 59–63
caladium, 135
calibrachoa, 83
carbon sequestering, 84
carrots, 125, 139
cast iron plant, 131
celery, 39, 97, 101, 113
chamomile, German, 143
chemicals
    culinary gardens and, 113–114
    dangers of, 29–30
    and health, 114
    soil and, 32
Chicago Botanic Garden, *12, 18, 19*
Chinese evergreen, 107, 131
chives, 39, 113

chrysanthemum, 107
cilantro, 37, 43–44, 52, 98, 101,
    113, 139
cleome, 144
coleus, 79, 89, 135
collard greens, 39, 51–52, 97, 139
colony collapse disorder, 73
color, *18*, 36, 38, 135–136
Colorful Living Wall, 135–137
companion planting, 149
compost, 32, *32*, 149–151
compost tea, *34*, 34
containers, 16
coreopsis, 83
Crassula ovata, 93
creeping jenny, *66*, 135
cucumber, 101, 102, 125
culinary gardens
    Culinary Kitchen Garden, 113–117
    locations for, 113–114
    Vitamin-Rich Culinary Garden,
        139–141
Culinary Kitchen Garden, 113–117
cultivators, 26

dandelion, 52
deformed wing virus (DWV), 74
design
    aphrodisiac gardens and, 102
    color and, *18*, 36, 38, 135–136
    insulating walls and, *87*
    starting from seed and, 125
    vegetables and, 97
disease, 148
Dracaenas, 107, 131
dragon wing begonia, 135
drainage
    cactus and, 61
    for insulation gardens, 84
    recycled materials and, 90
    soil and, 38, 56
    succulents and, 94
drinking-safe water hoses, 27
drought tolerance, 143–144
dry moss, 47–49
dusty miller, 144

EarthBox gardening systems, 144
Echeveria elegans, 93
Echiveria pulvinata, 93
ecowalls. *See* living walls
endive, 39
energy efficiency, 9, 10, 13, 55, 83–87

English ivy, 107
essential oils, 119
Euphorbia, Diamond Frost, 144

felt wrap living walls, 24
fennel, 39, 101, 102, 119
Fern Garden, 55–57
ferns, 55–57, *57*
fertilizers, 29–30, *34*, 34, 37, 56, 148
flowering tobacco, 119
flowers
    drought-tolerant varieties, 144
    edible, *19*
    scented, 119
    using, 43
food pantries, 37
Forrester Research, 132
Freestanding Entrance Garden,
    107–111
fruits, 38, 39
fungicides, 29–30, 73

garbage, 89. *See also* recycling
gardening, benefits of, 10–12
geraniums, scented, 119, 121
Gerbera daisy, 107
golden creeping jenny, 135
golden pothos, 107

hardening off, 36
heat island effect, 10, 74
hens-and-chicks, 93
Herbal Cocktail Garden, 43–45
herbicides, 29–30
herbs
    for aphrodisiac garden, 101
    for aromatherapy gardens, 119
    for culinary gardens, 113
    drought-tolerant varieties, 144
    harvesting, 44, 45
    as ornamental plants, 38, 39
    as oxygenators, 51–52
    pollinators and, 37
    for therapeutic gardens, 65
    using, 43
    vitamin content of, 140
homemade systems, 22-24, *25*.
    See also recycling
hoses, 27
houseplants, 107–108, 131
Hydroponic Pollinator Garden, 73–77
hydroponic systems, 23, 24, 73–77

impatiens, 79, 89
infusions, 43–44
Insulate-a-Wall Garden, 83–87
insulation, 83–87
irrigation systems, 31, 99, 109–111, 143

jade plant, 93
jellies, 44

*Journal of Environmental
    Psychology*, 131

kale
    for aphrodisiac garden, 101, 102
    for culinary gardens, 113
    'Dwarf Blue Curled', 39
    'Italian Lacinato Nero Toscana', 39
    as ornamental plant, 37–39, 83, 135
    as oxygenator, 51–52
    'Redbor', 38–39
    from seed, 125
    shady conditions and, 89, 135
    small-space gardening and, 97
    vitamin content of, 139
    'Winterbore', 39

Lampranthus blandus, 93
landscape fabric, 80
lantana, 73, 83, 144
lavender, 39, 43, 44, 73, 119
lemon balm, 119
lettuce, 39, 51–52, 89, 97–98, 113, 125
licorice plant, 83
light exposure, 29. *See also*
    shade; sunlight
lima beans, 139
living walls
    benefits of, 7–10, 19
    defined, 8
    purposes for, 13
    styles of, 24
    synonyms for, 8
    weight of, 24
lobelia, 89
Longwood Gardens Conservatory,
    11, 16
loose medium systems, 22, 23
love-in-a-mist, 125

marigold, 37
Mason jars, 68–69
mat systems, 22–23
medicine plant, 93, 107
microclimates, 30
microgreens, 39
mildew, 31
mint
    for aphrodisiac garden, 101
    chocolate, 83
    for culinary/cocktail gardens,
        43–44, 113
    as ornamental plant, 37, 39
    as oxygenator, 51–52
    for pollinator gardens, 73
    shady conditions and, 89
    small-space gardening and, 97
    for therapeutic gardens, 65
    modular planters/bracket styles, 24
    mondo grass, 135
Money-Saving Garden, 125–129

mood, 120–121
mosquito screens, 111
moss, 47–48
Moss and Shade Wall Art, 47–49
Mossandstonegardens.com, 47
municipal waste, 89. *See also* recycling
mustard greens, 39, 52, 139

nasturtium, 37, 43, 44, 89, 125
National Aeronautics and Space
    Administration (NASA), 108, 131
neonicotinoids, 36
New Guinea impatiens, 79, 89, 135
nicotiana, 73
noise reduction, 13, 83
nutrition, 101–102, 139–140

oregano
    'Amethyst Falls', 39
    for aromatherapy gardens, 119
    for culinary gardens, 113
    drought tolerance of, 143
    Greek, 43, 73
    as oxygenator, 52
    shady conditions and, 89
    small-space gardening and, 97
    for therapeutic gardens, 65, *66*
    'Variegated', 39
    vitamin content of, 139
ornamental cabbage, 39
ornamental hot peppers, 39
ornamental kale, 39
oxalis, 144

pallets, 13, 79–81
pansy, 37
parsley, 52, 97–98, 101–102, 113, 139
peace lily, 107, 131
peas, 139
Pelargonium tomentosum
    'Chocolate Mint', 121
Pelargonium tomentosum
    'Peppermint', 121
peony, 43, 44
peperomia, 131
peppermint, 43
peppers, 39, 97, 139, 143
perennials, 39
pesticides, 29–30
pests, 29–30, 149
philodendron, 107, 131
phthalates, 31
pink vygie, 93
planting pockets, 70–71
plants
    ecological concerns in choosing,
        35–36
    maintenance of, 148
    starting from seed, 36
    sun requirements of, 29
    watering needs and, 31

pleurocarpous moss, 47
plush plant, 93
pocket systems, *22*, 23–24
pollinators, 7–8, 13, 36–37, 73–74, 84
polka dot plant, 135
pothos, 107, 131
potting scoops, 26
pruners, *27*, 27
purple basil, 37
purple kohlrabi, 39

radicchio, 39
radishes, 125
rain barrels, 31
rain wands, 27, *28*, 143
recycling, 13, *22*, 23–24, 47, 79, 89–90
rhubarb, 39, 143
root systems, *30*
rose, 43
rosemary, 39, 43, 65, *66*, 119, 139
row markers, *28*, 28
Royal College of Agriculture
    (Circencester, England), 131

sage, 73, 143
salvia, 73
savory, winter, 143
scent, 67, 102, 119–123
scissors, *27*, 27
Sedum acre, 93
Sedum morganianum, 93
sedums, *18*
seed starting, 28, 36, 125–126
self-watering containers, 144
Sempervivum tectorum, 93
Senecio Spp., 93
shade
    Fern Wall Garden, 55–57
    geraniums and, 121
    low-light houseplants, 131
    plants for, 79, 89, 135
    Shade Pallet Garden, 79–81
Shade Pallet Garden, 79–81
Smart Garden, 131–133
Smell and Taste Treatment and
    Research Foundation, 102
snake plant, 107, 131
snapdragon, 37, 43, 89
soil
    for cactus, 61
    chemicals and, 32–33
    for Fern Wall Garden, 55, 56
    for insulation gardens, 84–85
    loose medium systems and, 23
    ornamental edibles and, 38
    plants and correct, 30
    recipes for, 33
    for succulents, 94
sorrel, 52
Spanish daisy, 73
spider plants, 79, 107, 131

spinach, 38, 39, 51, 89, 113, 125,
    139, 143
standalone systems, 52
stonecrop, 93
storm water management, 83–84
strawberries, 39
Succulent Living Wall, 93–95
succulents
    plant choices, 93
    soil for, 33
    sunlight and, 93–94
    temperature and, 93–94
    watering needs, 31, 108
    See also cactus
sunflowers, mini, 125
sunlight, 29, 61, 93–94
sweet peas, 125
sweet potato, 139
sweet potato vine, 39, *44*, 79, 83,
    89, 135
Swiss chard
    for aphrodisiac garden, 101, 102
    'Bright Lights', 83
    for culinary gardens, 113
    drought tolerance of, 143
    as ornamental plant, 37–39
    as oxygenator, 51–52
    from seed, 125
    shady conditions and, 89, 135
    small-space gardening and, 97
    vitamin content of, 139

tarragon, Mexican, 39
Therapeutic Fabric Pocket Garden,
    70–71
therapeutic gardens, 13, 65, 67, 68–71
Therapeutic Mason Jar Garden, 68–69
thyme
    for aromatherapy gardens, 119
    for culinary gardens, 113
    drought tolerance of, 143
    'Golden Lemon', 39
    lemon, 39, 43, 65, 119
    silver, 39
    small-space gardening and, 97
    for therapeutic gardens, 65
tillandsia, 11
tomatoes, 38, 97, 143
tools, 26–28
torenia, 135
toxins, 27, 31, 114
trap cropping, 149
trimming, 148
tropical plants, *18*, 36–37
trowels, 26
turnip greens, 52, 102
turnips, 97

University of Illinois Urbana-Champaign
    Landscape and Human Health
    Laboratory, 51, 135

upcycling. *See* recycling
Urban Water-Saving Garden, 143–147
utility expenses, 7, 10

Vegetable "Balconies" Garden, 51–53
vegetables
    for aphrodisiac gardens, 101
    for culinary gardens, 113
    design and, 97
    drought-tolerant varieties, 144
    fertilizers and, 34, 37, 38
    harvesting, 97
    heirloom, 36
    microclimates and, 30
    nutrient content, 13
    as ornamental plants, 38–39
    as oxygenators, 51–52
    small spaces and, 97–98
    vitamin content of, 139–140
    watering needs of, 31
verbena, 73, 83, 144
Vertical Vegetable Farm, 97–99
violet, 43
Vitamin-Rich Culinary Garden,
    139–141
vitamins, 139–140

walls
    insulations of, 83–87
    locating/placing, *20*, 29, 30
    strength of, 24
wall sculptures, 48–49
wall styles, 24
wall systems, types of, *22*, 22–23, *23*
water conservation, 13, 143–147
watercress, 52, 139
watering
    of acrocarpous moss, 48
    cactus and, 61
    gardens to minimize, 143–144
    options for, 31
    ornamental edibles and, 38
    succulents and, 94, 108
    techniques, 31
    time of day and, 31
    tools for, 27–28
    wall strength and, 24
watering cans, 28
watering wands, 27, *28*
weeders, 26
weeding, 8
window boxes systems, 23, 24
worm castings, 32, *34*, 149–150

Xel-Ha Eco-Park (Mexico), *14*

Zee Zee plant, 131
zinnia, 73, 125

MEET SHAWNA CORONADO

SHAWNA IS AN AUTHOR, columnist, blogger, professional photographer, spokesperson, and keynote speaker specializing in green lifestyle living, organic gardening, and culinary topics who campaigns for social good. She is also an on-camera spokesperson and social media personality. Shawna's garden has been featured in many venues, including PBS television, WGN TV News, and all over the web. Her organic living photographs and stories have been shown both online and off in many international home and garden magazines and multiple books. Meet Shawna by connecting online at her blog and website at www.shawnacoronado.com.